DISRUPTIVE POWER

OXFORD STUDIES IN DIGITAL POLITICS

Series Editor: Andrew Chadwick, Royal Holloway, University of London

DISRUPTIVE POWER

THE CRISIS OF THE STATE IN THE DIGITAL AGE

TAYLOR OWEN

OXFORD
UNIVERSITY PRESS

OXFORD

UNIVERSITY PRESS

Oxford University Press is a department of the University of Oxford.
It furthers the University's objective of excellence in research, scholarship,
and education by publishing worldwide.

Oxford   New York
Auckland   Cape Town   Dar es Salaam   Hong Kong   Karachi
Kuala Lumpur   Madrid   Melbourne   Mexico City   Nairobi
New Delhi   Shanghai   Taipei   Toronto

With offices in
Argentina   Austria   Brazil   Chile   Czech Republic   France   Greece
Guatemala   Hungary   Italy   Japan   Poland   Portugal   Singapore
South Korea   Switzerland   Thailand   Turkey   Ukraine   Vietnam

Oxford is a registered trade mark of Oxford University Press
in the UK and certain other countries.

Published in the United States of America by
Oxford University Press
198 Madison Avenue, New York, NY 10016

Library of Congress Cataloging-in-Publication Data
Owen, Taylor.
Disruptive power : the crisis of the state in the digital age / Taylor Owen.
    p.   cm. — (Oxford studies in digital politics)
ISBN 978-0-19-936386-5 (hardback)
1. Technology and international relations. 2. Internet and international relations.
I. Title.
JZ1254.O84 2015
327—dc23

2014034687

1   3   5   7   9   8   6   4   2

Printed in the United States of America on acid-free paper

"To: R & W"

CONTENTS

ACKNOWLEDGMENTS

This book represents the culmination of three meandering years exploring the intersection of digital technology and international affairs and is ultimately the product of many people's work. It began as a lecture and working paper for the Trudeau Foundation in the spring of 2012, and I am appreciative of PG Forest giving me the chance to come back to the Foundation and try out some new ideas on the smartest (and most critical) crowd in Canada. At the time, the ideas presented were nascent, and represented my initial explorations of what I increasingly saw as the profound ways technology was reshaping the international system.

This essay became a larger research project funded by a Social Sciences and Humanities Research Council grant called International Relations in the Digital Age, a partnership between the Canadian International Council and UBC. My friend and colleague Anouk Dey was critical as an RA on both of these initial stages. And my co-PI on the SSHRC research project, partner at the CIC and Open-Canada and close friend Jennifer Jeffs built the project and team with me. We had a great group of UBC journalism students helping out with a wide range of research, including Sadiya Ansari, Lindsay Sample, Kate Adach, Alexis Beckett, and Alexandra Gibb.

For the year I spent focusing on researching and writing the book, I had the amazing good fortune of having two wonderful RA's, Tanzeel Hakak and Cherise Seucharan. Both are wise beyond their years, and handled my ridiculous schedule and wandering (they would say vague) ideas with grace and persistence. Many of the ideas in this book are theirs as much as mine.

While writing this book I was also working at the Tow Center for Digital Journalism at Columbia with the extraordinary and tolerant Emily Bell. The incredible opportunities that working with Emily on building the Tow Center afforded me, as well as the time she allowed me to binge write among the cramming undergrads in the Bodleian, made this book possible.

As I have now learned, bringing a book into the world is a process. Three people made this one happen. First, Ethan Bassoff at Lippincott Massie McQuilkin took a chance on me, and got this book into the hands of New York publishers. Second, Angela Chnapko at Oxford University Press was supportive, encouraging, and incredibly helpful at every stage of the editing and publishing process. Finally, Blake Eskin agreed to dive in to the project as an utterly ruthless editor, and gave me the most educational writing experience I have ever had.

Finally, and by far most importantly, I owe everything to my amazing parents and to my best friend, confidant, fiercest critic, partner and wife Ariel, and to our little man Walter.

DISRUPTIVE POWER

CHAPTER ONE

LOSING CONTROL

Information is power. But like all power, there are those who want to keep it for themselves.

—Aaron Swartz

In January 2012, the Federal Bureau of Investigation (FBI), Scotland Yard, and intelligence agencies in Italy, France, the Netherlands, Denmark, and Sweden created a task force to counter Anonymous. These countries saw the collective of activist hackers and its numerous offshoots as a national security threat.

Anonymous—which is best defined as an Internet gathering with a loose and decentralized command structure that operates on ideas rather than directives[1]—came to prominence in 2008 when it mounted an attack on the Church of Scientology's website after the church asked YouTube to take down a video interview with Tom Cruise. Anonymous saw the takedown as an act of censorship and said it wanted to completely remove the Church of Scientology's presence on the Internet and to "save people from Scientology by reversing the brainwashing." Since then, hundreds of digital actions have been undertaken in the name of Anonymous, ebbing and flowing in both scale and frequency. The group has inserted itself into political conflicts in the United States and around the globe.

In November 2011, at an Occupy rally against budget cuts and increased tuition at the University of California, San Diego, a riot police officer was filmed pepper-spraying a peaceful protestor. When video of the incident went viral on YouTube, Anonymous responded by leaking the police officer's name, address, phone number, and email address. He received over 17,000 threatening emails, 10,000 text messages, and hundreds of letters. The group did the same to Arizona Department of Public Safety officials in response to the passage of Arizona Bill 1070, an anti-immigration bill widely seen as racist. This attack was part of the bigger operation called Anti-Sec in which Anonymous attacked many Western governments for reasons ranging from Internet censorship to racial profiling.

During the Arab Spring, Anonymous worked in support of anti-government protestors in Tunisia, Egypt, and Libya, hacking into government websites, shutting them down with distributed denial-of service (DDoS) attacks, and releasing names, email addresses, and passwords of government officials. In December of 2011, in the name of revealing corporate and government corruption, Anonymous hacked into the US intelligence consultancy Stratfor, obtaining, among other data, 2.7 million corporate emails detailing often sensitive conversations involving current and former government officials and thousands of off-the-record sources.

While these operations have many common objectives and use similar hacking tactics, Anonymous is hard to pin down. It has no fixed leadership and no national affiliation. Individuals loosely coordinate, then attribute their actions to Anonymous. As one hacker who participates in Anonymous told a Baltimore journalist, "We have this agenda that we all agree on and we all coordinate and act, but all act independently toward it, without any want for recognition. We just want to get something that we feel is important done."[2]

Describing Anonymous is a challenge when writing a book. For an intelligence agency—and particularly one like the FBI, which has a history of combating perceived US threats ranging from the Communist Party to al-Qaeda—its amorphous structure, mandate, and tactics can cause much greater concern. The United States, which created the Internet as a defense research project, now considers cyberspace a "domain" or potential battlefield equal in importance to land, sea, air, and outer space. As a result, Anonymous and other groups involved in cyberattacks are seen as actors who need to be controlled. But Anonymous does not work like other political or military actors. It does not use accepted international conventions of protest—political marches, petitions, physical violence—to pursue its goals.

It does not need to. Over the past decade, rapid advances in digital technology have empowered individuals and ad hoc groups to do what was once available only to institutions run by the state and to private organizations built on a similar top-down, bureaucratic model. "Anonymous demonstrates one of the new core aspects of power in a networked, democratic society: individuals are vastly more effective and less susceptible to manipulation, control, and suppression by traditional sources of power than they were even a decade ago,"

Yochai Benkler, a professor at Harvard's Berkman Center for Internet and Society, wrote in 2012 in *Foreign Affairs*.[3] As will be explored in these pages, individuals can now do things that replace and threaten existing institutions in all areas of international affairs, including: development, war, diplomacy, finance, international reporting, and activism.

And intelligence gathering: On January 13, 2012, when FBI agent Timothy Lauster wrote to task force members to set up a conference call "to discuss the on-going investigations related to Anonymous, Lulzsec, Antisec, and other associated splinter groups,"[4] Donncha O'Cearrbhail, a 19-year-old from Offaly County, Ireland, intercepted his email. The next day, O'Cearrbhail asked a prominent Anonymous activist known as Sabu for help over Internet Relay Chat, a text-based messaging system. "I have acquired info about the time, phone number, and pin number of the conference call," O'Cearrbhail wrote. "I just don't have a good VoIP (Voice Over Internet Protocol) setup for actually calling in to record it."[5]

O'Cearrbhail got help. On January 17, he recorded the conference call. He sent the file to Sabu, and when Sabu failed to post the recording, an audio file was posted on YouTube on February 3, which a well-followed anonymous-linked twitter handle @AnonymousIRC promoted and then tweeted: "The #FBI might be curious how we're able to continuously read their internal comms for some time now #OpInfiltration."[6]

This act of transparency did not go unpunished. O'Cearrbhail did not know that Sabu was an FBI informant, enabling criminal hacking under agency guidance. The US government had five individuals involved with the conference call arrested, including O'Cearrbhail, and charged them with computer hacking conspiracy, computer hacking, and intentionally disclosing an unlawfully intercepted wire communication. O'Cearrbhail was ultimately released without charge. Other Anonymous members, including alleged leaders of the movement, have also been detained. Still, the network continues to grow and to challenge the authority of democracies and autocratic states.

———

In international affairs, the term "rogue" is applied to states such as Iran and North Korea, which disregard the norms of the international system. It has also been applied to al-Qaeda, which seeks to destroy Middle Eastern and Western governments and restore an international Muslim caliphate of the sort that existed in the centuries after Mohammed. In short, a rogue actor is one who isn't constrained by existing controls on behavior. A state, for example, can be belligerent, even violent, but do so within the bounds of international law and accepted norms of behavior. States can be constrained by the same methods. It is when an actor is perceived as uncontrollable that it gets the label of rogue.

Is Anonymous a rogue group? Yochai Benkler argues that Anonymous, unlike al-Qaeda, "causes disruption, not destruction." DDoS attacks on websites have not changed the Vatican's stance on abortion or overturned the government of Bahrain, but the line between destruction and disruption is largely subjective. As cybercrime author Richard Powers observes, Anonymous is "attacking the whole power structure"—the international economic and political systems that have developed over the past century.[7] Like many of the individuals and organizations innovating online, Anonymous confounds the institutions, boundaries, and categories that have maintained the balance of power since the end of World War II. Considering that the nation-state has the most to lose, and has in the past maintained its control via the institutions now being disrupted, governmental concern is understandable.

Rogue or not, Anonymous is not an anomaly, and taking its leaders out of circulation will not stop it or like-minded groups. It represents an early example of a new form of digitally derived power that is disrupting a wide range of once powerful 21st-century institutions, not just in international affairs.

Disruption has become one of Silicon Valley's most popular, if cloying, buzzwords. One is hard pressed to find a startup that does not describe itself as a disruptive technology, or a company founder who is reluctant to take on the establishment. The concept has also come to stand for a form of libertarianism deeply rooted in the technology sector, a sweeping ideology that goes well beyond the precept that technology can engage social problems to the belief that free market technology-entrepreneurialism should be left unhindered by the state. In a sense then, Anonymous is an ideological manifestation of the most doctrinaire of the new technology elite. It represents the anarchistic end of a spectrum that includes everything from the belief that private-sector massive open online courses extend the benefits of higher education to more radical notions of markets unencumbered by taxes and regulation and offshore islands free from the control of the state. At one end is the hope that technology can make our social and governance systems more efficient. On the other is a desire to burn down the house—to take down the state.

The concept of disruption is rooted in the work of Clay Christensen, a professor of business administration at the Harvard Business School who was originally interested in why unimpressive technologies, like the transistor radio, allow upstarts like Sony to take over markets from established companies like RCA and Zenith, with their refined product lines and large markets. "Why is it that companies like these invest aggressively and successfully in the technologies necessary to retain their current customers but then fail to make certain other technological investments that customers of the future will demand?" Christensen asked in a 1995 *Harvard Business Review* article written with colleague Joseph Bower.[8] The authors argue that well-established companies are ahead in developing new technologies that meet the needs of established customers, but they cannot see beyond the worldview that made them successful. This blind spot allows new companies to innovate on the margins. Disruptive technologies first find a niche audience, and once their value is proven, they widen their market, taking down the establishment. In short, hierarchical institutions with entrenched practices, interests, and consumers are bad at anticipating and catering to new markets and are therefore vulnerable to nimble innovators.

Christensen wrote a series of influential books, beginning with *The Innovator's Dilemma*, which look at many industries, including airlines, steel mills, and journalism, through the prism of disruption theory.[9] He has also applied disruption theory to the public sector. In a 2006 article Christensen and his co-authors argued that in the United States too much social spending is directed at maintaining the status quo rather than at reaching underserved populations. "Catalytic innovation," they write, would "challenge industry incumbents by offering simpler, good-enough alternatives to an underserved group of customers."[10]

Government has all the burdens of established corporations: institutionalized structures and norms that lead to lethargy, waste, inefficiency, and a lack of innovation. But their purpose is different from that of corporations, which have a mission to maximize value for their shareholders. In the capitalist model, we hope that the collective impact of the private sector benefits everyone to some extent. In the public sector, however, the very mandate is to serve everyone. Disruption theory explains the failure of institutions to innovate and their risks of collapse, not the social consequence of that failure. The Kodak workers who lost jobs, or towns where the steel mills closed, are not the core focus of business theory. And herein lies the problem for the state.

Disruptive innovation—from Anonymous, to cryptocurrencies like Bitcoin, to grassroots mapping of natural disasters—is challenging many core functions of the international system, functions once controlled by states and international institutions. The difference, of course, is that the state won't go away so easily, and the costs of disrupting it can be very

8

high. A Foreign Ministry or Defense Department suffers from the same institutional constraints outlined by Christensen, yet it cannot creatively destruct. Or if it does, the risks are enormous, because disruptive innovation could signal the end of the centuries-long modes of state governance. And despite the imaginings of the techno- and crypto-anarchists, the repercussions would be vast. So the stakes are high, and the aspects of the state's traditional power are fundamentally threatened.

For now, the challenge posed by disruptive innovation does not mean the end of the state, but it does suggest that the state is in decline, exposing laws, ethics, norms of behavior, and hierarchical structures that emerged amid an older set of technologies as constraints. Put another way, the state is losing its status as the pre-eminent mechanism for collective action. Where it used to be that the state had a virtual monopoly on the ability to shape the behavior of large numbers of people, this is no longer the case. Enabled by digital technology, disruptive innovators are now able to influence the behavior of large numbers of people without many of the societal constraints that have developed around state action. These constraints, which disruption theory treats as weaknesses, have historically been strengths of democratic societies: They hold government accountable and ensure that it operates within the rule of law and within the bounds of prevailing moral and ethical norms. There are of course varying degrees of success within this framework, but the idea of collective representation via institutional governance is what has separated modern democratic societies from anarchy.

What does it mean to disrupt the state? What does disruptive innovation look like in the world of international relations? And how is the modern state, still with tremendous power and capacity for violence, pushing back against disruptions?

———

It is widely understood, while sometimes overstated, that the Arab Spring movements in Tunisia, Libya, and Egypt were enabled in part by the use of digital technology and social media. Protestors, traditional media, and citizen journalists all used Internet-based technologies to organize events, coordinate movement, and broadcast their activities to the watching world.

What was less clear at the time, but is now evident, is that the autocratic regimes that they were protesting were digitally equipped to fight back. Egyptian president Hosni Mubarak sought to shut down the Internet, and Bahrain has proven to be adept at monitoring and censoring its citizens. Nowhere, however, was this digital capability more evident than in Syria, where a government was willing to brutally kill tens if not hundreds of thousands of its citizens to halt the spread of protests from North Africa. Syria, led by President Bashar Assad, has almost total control over the telecommunication of its citizens. At a national level, state-owned Syrian Telecommunication Establishment censored and filtered communications to crack down on protestors, activists, and the main rebel organization, the Free Syrian Army. In parallel to government initiatives, a network of hackers calling themselves the Syrian Electronic Army operates in general support of Assad, both in Syria and globally—for example, hacking the AP Twitter feed and claiming that the White House has been bombed, causing a $136.5 billion drop in the S&P 500. Both the state and its allied hackers use sophisticated technologies to track and target anti-government protestors.

Where do an autocratic regime and its supporters get such technology? In Syria's case, the Assad regime obtained devices manufactured by Blue Coat Systems, a California company. A research center at the University of Toronto called the Citizen Lab uncovered this connection after obtaining a set of log files from these devices. (After initial denials, Blue Coat acknowledged that its devices were being used in Syria, but denied that the company sold them directly to the Syrian government, which would violate a US Executive Order banning the transfer to Iran and Syria of technologies that facilitate computer or network disruption, monitoring, or tracking.) The Citizen Lab later showed that more than twenty other countries, including a long list of rights abusers such as Egypt, Saudi Arabia, Afghanistan, Bahrain, China, Iraq, Nigeria, Russia, and Venezuela, also use Blue Coat devices to censor or monitor Internet activity.[11] The US government is also a Blue Coat customer and used its devices to block Pentagon access to websites supporting gay rights from Department of Defense computers.[12]

Blue Coat is hardly the only Western corporation to provide surveillance services to autocratic regimes. Google engineers in Egypt discovered contract proposals from a digital security software company called Gamma International to the Mubarak regime for €250,000 worth of technology that would "enable them to intercept dissidents' emails, record audio and video chats, and take copies of computer hard drives."[13] High-profile technology companies such as Gamma and FinSpy supplied surveillance services to regimes in Egypt, Tunisia, Libya, Bahrain, and Syria. An operation by WikiLeaks and the British non-governmental organization (NGO) Privacy International revealed 287 documents indicating that surveillance companies, such as the French arms dealer Amesys, sold both spyware and malware to Gaddafi in Libya.[14] Narus, a US-based Boeing subsidiary, sold surveillance equipment to Egypt, and Trovicor, a German company, did the same for a dozen Middle Eastern and North African countries.[15]

Five times a year, hundreds of vendors come together in Prague, Dubai, Brasilia, Washington, and Kuala Lumpur to sell upward of $5 billion in tracking, censoring, monitoring, and spying technology at the Intelligent Support Systems trade show, also known as the Wiretappers Ball.[16] These events attract the arms and surveillance industries, blue-chip corporations, and officials from democratic and autocratic governments alike. A 2012 event brought together more than 2,700 representatives from 110 countries, including problematic regimes in Afghanistan, Belarus, and Sudan.[17] When asked whether he would be comfortable with Zimbabwe and North Korea buying technology there, Jerry Lucas, who runs the Wiretappers Ball, told the *Guardian*, "That's just not my job to determine who's a bad country and who's a good country. Do some countries use this technology to suppress political statements? Yes, I would say that's probably fair to say. But who are the vendors to say that the technology is not being used for good as well as for what you would consider not so good?"[18]

————

Jerry Lucas is hardly the only one who expects autocratic regimes to use such technology to spy on citizens. In fact, as the Assad regime was monitoring dissent, the US State Department was developing an ambitious project to "arm" opposition members with surveillance-circumvention technology.

During the 2009–2010 Iranian "green revolution" protests, the concept of Internet freedom became a buzzword in Washington. By the time of the Arab Spring revolutions, the State Department was ready to help to develop and provide new digital tools to dissidents. Via a $57 million congressional allocation, and as a part their wider 21st-century statecraft initiative, the department developed programs to train and equip allies in the region with anonymizing and circumvention tools.[19]

One such project was called the Internet in a Suitcase, which uses cellphones and wifi routers to create distributed networks that allow for secure communication. During the 2012 Internet outage where Assad effectively shut down all cellphone and Internet activity, approximately 2,000 of these mesh network kits were distributed to opposition members.[20] "The United States is going beyond humanitarian aid and providing additional assistance, including communications equipment that will help activists organize, evade attacks by the regime, and connect to the outside world," Secretary of State John Kerry said.[21]

This means that the US State Department is providing circumvention tools (technology the FBI has labeled an "indicator of terrorist activity") to dissidents who are being targeted by a government armed with digital surveillance tools made in the United Nations. As Sascha Meinrath, who is leading the Internet in a Suitcase project, says, "a lot of these technologies can be used for great good, but they are also a Faustian bargain."[22]

States now find themselves in a convoluted position, as both enablers and targets of disruptive actors. And this perfectly represents the complexity of power, agency, and control on the Internet. This Faustian bargain is a manifestation of a new arms race, between people who are empowered through free, secure communication and governments that want to monitor and limit this communication. But it also tells us something about the way the state views, and is increasingly reacting to, the capabilities of digital technology and to those that are empowered by them.

Until the summer of 2013, this tension was the focus of my research for this book. Digital technology, I hypothesized, was enabling nontraditional international actors to take on and in some important ways replace the capacity of states and large institutions in ways that were both filled with opportunity but also fundamentally destabilizing to the established international order. States were taking notice and began to play the delicate game of both supporting and in some cases even funding what they perceived as beneficial disruptive behavior (economic innovation, Syrian dissidents) while at the same time cracking down on disruptions perceived as threatening (Anonymous, terrorist communication, the black market).

What I didn't know, which we now do, is that in the wake of September 11,[23] Western democratic governments were so concerned about the capabilities of the digitally empowered that they became willing to subvert these digital powers and reassert their control over communications. We have now learned both how threatened the state truly was and the extent they were willing to go to control individuals and groups they perceived as nefarious actors. This book then also became a study of how democratic states were using technology and the consequences of a digital arms race between states and their citizens.

When Edward Snowden, an American defense contractor based in Hawaii, leaked a vast trove of documents detailing the National Security Agency's (NSA) surveillance program, the breadth and audacity of the US surveillance state shocked the world. Snowden provided data that explained how the United States and other democracies were attempting to control as much of the global telecommunications system as possible. In a chilling graphic presented to a meeting of the "Five Eyes" surveillance alliance (made up of the United Kingdom, the United States, Canada, Australia, and New Zealand) the NSA described their "New Collection Posture." The operational goals were summarized in a mantra: "Collect it All; Process it All; Exploit it All; Partner it All; Sniff it All; Know it All."[24] A similar document from British Government Communications Headquarters describes a satellite communications surveillance program as a "Collect it All proof-of-concept system." A memo from the NSA to Japan brags that new capabilities are "bringing our enterprise one step closer to collecting it all."[25]

The underlying military rationale for the surveillance state is rooted in the mentality that one can control a battlefield through situational awareness. The more one knows, the more one can control outcomes. Digital omniscience is incredibly difficult to accomplish, however, and it could ultimately break a technological system, the Internet, that is paradoxically the source of enormous personal freedom, expression, and empowerment.

For the state to collect everything, to "know it all," it must first normalize pervasive surveillance. Because al-Qaeda shares many of the attributes of disruptive innovators, 9/11 afforded democratic states the pretext to pass sweeping security legislation. The state's appetite for omniscience is of course not new, but we now know that the Patriot Act, drafted in a matter of days and passed by Congress with only a single dissenting voice, enabled a vast global surveillance infrastructure. As journalist Quinn Norton notes, the security establishment can succumb to paranoia as well as self-preservation: "When you're an incredibly well-funded defense and intelligence community, the lack of existential threats is an existential threat. There is nothing to do but be scared of things."[26]

And this is partly for good reason: Al-Qaeda posed a new kind of threat. Its constituent parts were decentralized, spread out around the world, based on an idea, and despite their unconventional use of weaponry, connected and fueled by their ability to communicate, both clandestinely and in the media. They were not a national army that could be defeated on a traditional battlefield. They have also proved technologically adept. In the summer of 2014, analysis demonstrated how they have responded to increased state surveillance by developing their own encryptions tools.[27]

This fear coincided with an additional cultural, technological, and economic development: the creation of vast amounts of data encompassing human communication and movement. Google's mission is to organize the world's information, a project that is rapidly growing to include the use of robotic data collection, satellite footage, drones, and artificial intelligence. Facebook seeks to connect everyone in the world, and in so doing has detailed social and behavioral data on over a billion people. It is developing advanced facial recognition and moving into virtual reality.

There is a perceived benign utopianism to these objectives that the state has been able to co-opt. Technology became pervasive enough for most people to use Internet-connected devices, corporations developed business models dependent on mining data from these communications, and citizens willingly (if not always consciously) exchanged their personal data for free online services. For a government that sought to know everything, to collect it all, corporations had built an infrastructure, and the public had filled in much of the data. The same technological system that empowers people to disrupt traditional and state institutions has been shown to be incredibly effective at providing the backbone of a surveillance state.

When Edward Snowden showed the extent, breadth, and audacity of the US surveillance state, he wasn't just revealing a program he saw as unconstitutional or unethical. He was providing the data required to understand how the US government had chosen to respond to the challenges of digitally empowered actors. Just as the Syrian government had chosen to use digital networks as a domain to control, the US government had, in a post 9/11 state of panic and fear, decided to exert power over the network itself. As Snowden himself says, "These programs were never about terrorism: they're about economic spying, social control, and diplomatic manipulation. They're about power."

———

Digital technology has empowered individuals and groups to do things that previously only states and large institutions could accomplish. Precisely those trends that have weakened the power of the state—and that states have thus been programmed to dissuade—have strengthened a new set of actors who are well placed to advance the rights and freedoms of individuals. But these networked actors are no more morally bound than those that operate within the traditional state system. They can use their power in many ways, for altruistic or malicious ends. It is therefore their ability to act and the new forms of action enabled by networked technology that are the primary focus of this book.

The digitally empowered are only part of the story. Threatened by this decentralized power and fearful of nefarious actors wielding it, the state is fighting back. Since digital technology challenges centralized command and hierarchical control, the state is increasingly seeking to control the network itself. But in attempting to limit digital empowerment, states could ultimately destroy the benefits and freedoms of the network. States will have to choose between seeking absolute control and giving up some power in order to preserve the emerging system. Democratic governments in particular face a dilemma, as the attributes that determine success in a networked world are ones that their institutions were built to dissuade. Increasingly, the capabilities of the state are at odds with its objectives. This tension is not sustainable.

This 21st-century foreign policy challenge is explored in three parts. The first part begins with *Disruptive Power*, tracing the development of the modern state, which began as a mechanism for centralizing and exercising power and became hierarchical, bureaucratic, and, in democratic states, accountable to the rule of law. In a networked world, however, groups like Anonymous wield power by being decentralized, collaborative, and resilient. This disruptive power threatens the institutions that have preserved the balance of power since the end of World War II.

The next four chapters look at individuals and groups fueled by digital technologies in ways that challenge the power of established institutions. *Spaces of Dissent* explores digital activism through the example of a group of hackers called Telecomix, who served as a form of tech support for the Arab Spring. *New Money* examines the rise of Bitcoin and what cryptocurrencies mean for the international financial system the state has long controlled. *Being There* considers the evolution of international reporting by juxtaposing the death of seasoned foreign war correspondent Marie Colvin during the bombing of Homs, Syria, with the new digital tools Syrian citizens used to document and stream the war to the world in real time. *Saving the Saviors* looks at the impact of collaborative mapping and advances in satellite technology on humanitarian and development agencies.

The final three chapters focus on the state's use of digital technology and its response to disruptive actors. The emerging practice of digital diplomacy—public diplomacy through social media as well as more invasive diplomatic initiatives—is the subject of *Diplomacy Unbound*. *The Violence of Algorithms* looks at how advances in computational power and automation have produced military weapons and surveillance tools that blur the boundaries of the battlefield and the lines between domestic and international. Finally, *The Crisis of the State* outlines four challenges that together threaten the state's traditional mechanisms of power and control, but that also might provide models for 20th-century international institutions seeking to adapt—if they are structurally capable of transformation or meaningful reform.

Digitally enabled actors, groups, and ad hoc networks are creating new forms of organization and often share different values and have conflicting objectives from the institutions of the current international system. What remains to be seen is whether the core characteristics of disruptive power are conducive to principles of accountability, stability, and democratic engagement, or fundamentally undermine them. In a world where the traditional state model empowers both democrats and dictators, this is not a new tension. But it is one that increasingly represents a crisis for both the state and the host of other 20th-century institutions that have long controlled power in the international system. At the start of a potentially long struggle for relevance, states will have to choose between seeking absolute control and giving up some power in order to preserve, and hopefully enhance, the emerging system.

CHAPTER TWO

DISRUPTIVE POWER

The modern history of power is inextricably tied to the development, interests, and capabilities of the state. The power that the state has accrued is derived from its ability to control its citizens, mobilize collective action, to regulate corporations and economic activity, and to influence other states. State power is hierarchical, institutional, and structural. It is also connected to the ability to control information and broadcasts. A contemporary discussion of foreign policy must move beyond the confines of state power, however, and into the nebulous, networked world emerging around us.

The rise of the nation-state as the primary unit of international politics coincides with the development of a new information technology. Gutenberg's printing press in the 15th century paved the way for a transition from the disaggregated feudal system of the Middle Ages to a more structured form of political power.

In addition to allowing information to be dispersed widely, the printing press shaped how information was conceived. To spread information, one had to put it in a linear, bound form. Society moved from a decentralized, oral tradition of knowledge-sharing with privileged access to books and literacy to one where information could be centralized, controlled, and mass-produced. And with this centralization of communicative and organizational authority came the modern state. This societal shift has largely determined the modern era. Some 350 years of governance, institutional design, political evolution, media, and culture have been dictated by humankind's rapport with the printed word.

The Treaty of Westphalia, signed in 1648, 200 years into the Gutenberg era, ended the Thirty Years' War and marks the birth of the modern nation-state system. Its core contribution was to establish principles for legitimate rule. These principles—sovereignty, the right of self-determination, legal equality between states, and nonintervention in the internal affairs of other states—would become norms for state behavior. A state's legitimacy was for the first time sanctioned by an interstate agreement.

The treaty also established what has been called a classic balance-of-power system, whereby large states were roughly considered equal, and wars of containment kept the system in check. Political scientist Alan C. Lamborn describes the goal of this system as preserving "the independence of the key states by preventing any one state from becoming so powerful militarily that it could dominate all the others."[1]

In the century before the Treaty of Westphalia, political philosophers were exploring the nature of power and social organization, looking at the bargains territorial states could make with their citizens and with other states. They were also publishing and widely distributing their ideas.

Machiavelli, in *The Prince*, and Hobbes, in *Leviathan*, argue that states gained power and legitimacy by protecting the security and well-being of their citizens. Fighting between states, they argued, could be minimized if the power and independence of each was mutually recognized.

Although there are multiple definitions of statehood, the generally used definition comes from Max Weber, who defines the state as "a human community that (successfully) claims the monopoly of the legitimate use of physical force within a given territory."[2] This basic notion of statehood implies that a legitimate state can use force against, or in favor of, its citizens without legal consequences.

Historians have identified two ways of looking at the state: Political philosophers such as Hobbes, Rousseau, and Locke held a Contractarian view of the state—that is, without the existence of the state (i.e., in the "state of nature"), there would be a foundation for anarchy and chaos everywhere. According to the Hobbesian idea of "war of every man against every man" in which life was "solitary, poor, nasty, brutish, and short," it is necessary to have a "common power to keep them all in awe."[3] This leads to the creation of a "social contract" or an implicit agreement among individuals to empower the state and follow rights and responsibilities vis-à-vis each other: "At some point in their history, certain peoples spontaneously, rationally, and voluntarily gave up their individual sovereignties and united with other communities to form a larger political unit deserving to be called a state."[4]

More contemporary definitions of statehood focus on the state as an organizational structure with a monopoly on the use of violence. Unlike the Contractarian view, which locates the source of the state in the conflict between individuals, the Predatory view focuses on conflict between the state and its citizens. In the Predatory view, the state uses its comparative advantage over the use of violence to enforce laws and rules upon its citizenry. This idea closely relates to that of sociologist Charles Tilly's notion of the "state as organized crime," in which the elites and the leaders work together to maintain the status quo by acquiring revenue and enforcing their power on the citizens. This view holds that the rulers of the state are egotistic, maximizing, rational actors who are interested in their own survival and thereby curtail whatever might appear as a threat to their monopoly over power. Tilly sees states as "relatively centralized, differentiated organizations, the officials of which, more or less, successfully claim control over the chief concentrated means of violence within a population inhabiting a large contiguous territory."[5] Economist Douglas North is even more direct: "A state is an organization with a comparative advantage in violence, extending over a geographic area whose boundaries are determined by its power to tax constituents."[6]

The primacy of control over the use of force is paramount in the Predatory view, but both have to do with the power of the state to control people. Internally, the state manifests its power via a social contract with its citizens, whereby it is seen to legitimately provide for the common good. And externally, it maintains power via the use or threat of force. Both of these forms of control are at their foundation, about power.

Has the power of the state declined? The 20th century saw the rise of the institutionalized and globalized state, and in many ways the end of the traditional empires and monarchist rule that had defined much of the previous centuries. Global powers fought two world wars to define the terms of this new global system. World War I essentially reversed the economic relationship between Europe and America. Whereas Britain and France had been the world's creditors, they became indebted to the United States. Following the war, the League of Nations was founded with the goal of bringing order and control to the state system. While ultimately without teeth, and thus ineffective at stopping World War II, it did lay the foundation for the United Nations.

Following World War II, once again, the result was more international institutionalization with the goal of mitigating the costs of state power. World leaders questioned the legitimacy of the state, appealing to universal principles of human rights and justice. This led to the founding of the United Nations to prevent another war between great powers. Perhaps the most consequential shift, and one that served to embed new powers with the state, were the financial institutions of the Bretton Woods agreement. This agreement implemented a largely free-market capitalist system for the global economy, with the state, and in particular the United States, at its center. The fixed exchange rate and gold standard systems were created, and the management of the international monetary system was placed in the International Monetary Fund. The International Trade Organization, later to become the General Agreement on

Tariffs and Trade, promoted movement toward a system of free trade between countries.

It is hard to imagine a more robust statement of state power than the creation of the global architecture that followed the two world wars. With it came the establishment of an international system with the United States and its economic model at the center. Beyond solidifying this power, the state-based institutions that were created were designed to address many of the world's problems.

This move to interstate institutions proved a double-edged sword for the nation-state. The success of the Bretton Woods institutions at liberalizing international trade inevitably led to globalization, which is undermining traditional core elements of state control, such as governance, populations, and territorial sovereignty. Whether it is the Internet's ability to transcend geographical boundaries or the rise of multinational corporations beyond the control of any one state, national governments have been challenged by new systems of power.[7] In their book *Globalization/Anti-Globalization*, David Held and Anthony McGrew argue that we are headed into a post-Westphalian system characterized by the increasing questioning of state sovereignty in subtle ways. New organizations and institutions are wielding authority that once belonged only to the state.[8]

Eminent international relations scholars Joseph Nye Jr. and Robert Keohane push back on such assessments.[9] The problem with such analyses, they argue, is that they underestimate the power of the state, which is more resilient and continues to command loyalty from a vast majority of citizens. These pundits of modernity, as Nye and Keohane call them, "failed to analyze how the holders of power could wield that power to shape or distort patterns of interdependence that cut across national boundaries."

What has been grossly overlooked, they argue, is how "the new world overlaps and rests on the traditional world in which power depends on geographically based institutions." They call the resulting landscape one of "complex interdependence," in which actors have multiple relationships depending on the nature of their interest, and each relationship is governed by some set of norms, values, and shared culture. This new ecosystem has not replaced state power, they argue, because "information does not flow in a vacuum but in political space that is already occupied." This is surely true, but it does not negate the possibility that power is indeed shifting, and that the power of the state could be diminishing.

Nor does it account for shifts in how the state itself wields power, an argument that Nye himself has championed through his theory of soft power. States, he argues, have two principal means of persuasion: the blunt force of military or economic coercion and the more subtle forms of coopting and attraction. In the latter, states make others want what they want through the promotion of their values—in the case of the United States, democracy, human rights, and individual prosperity. According to Nye, these values are promoted through a wide range of non-state institutions, and his concept of soft power has therefore come to be seen as a broadening of the mandate of the state into untraditional areas. While he still sees the state as the primary actor of the international system, the theory of soft power implicitly elevates a wide network of other groups and individuals who had previously been left out of the international conversation.

And they were about to get a lot more powerful. As international-relations scholars were beginning to theorize the changing role of the state, a revolution in information technology was under way. Digital information, and the forms of behavior which it allows, are unbound. Communications are no longer constrained by the linearity of print or the hierarchy of the 20th century, existing instead in fluid networks. They are emboldened by new attributes, such as anonymity and constant change.

What forms of power are emerging in this new space? And in what ways are scholars beginning to map out this new ecosystem of actors and technologies? One answer is the theory of networked power.

———

Networks are of course nothing new. Polynesian trade routes, the Hanseatic League, the Rothschild banks, African talking drummers were all non-hierarchical networks of nodes.

But thinking about them in an international relations context never seemed necessary because state power has been so hierarchical and dominant until recently. What's more, advances in information technology have vastly increased the importance of networks. A group of citizens could always organize an ad hoc protest, for example, but now this can be done quickly and on a vast scale with mobile phones over social networks.

Renowned communication theorist Manual Castells has in many ways pioneered the study of the social and policy effects of digital communication networks. He argues that digital technology enables different forms of behavior from what was possible on non-digital networks.[10]

In this view, digital technology increases the power of networks by overcoming the overwhelming challenges of coordination, communication, size, complexity, and velocity that previously limited networked behavior.[11]

States, Castells argues, are no longer isolated actors with enormous power. Their power is challenged and influenced by other powerful nodes, sub-networks, and alternative networks.[12] Beyond state behavior, network power has led to the re-creation of civil society at the global and the local levels. Despite the diversity of cultures and societies, networks knit civil society together. And this is also true at the personal level, where Castells sees a new form of networked individualism emerging. He describes a synthesis between our individual-centered culture and the desire to coexist online. Ultimately, for Castells, in a network society, power continues to be the fundamental structuring force. However, it does not reside in institutions, states, or corporations—rather, it is located in the network itself. And as such, it is the behavior within these networks that should be the object of our analysis.

In its simplest form, a network is a set of interconnected nodes (individual, groups, organizations, states, etc.) that allows the sharing of ideas, goods, values, and other resources. Networks produce patterns of relationships that influence those in and outside the network. Consequently, the power of a network is either derived from its internal structure or through the agency its structure derives.[13]

A network is an interplay between its structure and the actors that participate in it. Nodes in a social network can be analyzed as individual members, groups, or organizations; however, they are connected in ways that lead to dependency and patterns. Or, put another way, networks can have predictable, even determinative, structures akin to hierarchies.[14]

In computer science terms, nodes in a network have power because they can threaten to sever links with other nodes, giving them a degree of influence over their behavior.[15] As such, they can define the nature of the network by setting conditions and limitations on what information the other nodes are able to share. In this construct, powerful nodes emerge in part by reducing transaction costs of interacting within the network.

Actors within networks may view a network as a means for coordinated or collective action aimed at changing international outcomes and national policies. However, because these networks lack a formal legitimate organizational ability that would arbitrate or resolve disputes, and are non-hierarchical, have loose ties between nodes, and have less precise boundaries than traditional institutions, there is a fluidity to their behavior.

In *Here Comes Everybody: The Power of Organizing without Organizations*, technology theorist Clay Shirky sees networks as new formations of people and groups that in many ways sit outside the social organizations of hierarchical institutions. For Shirky, the word "organization" has several meanings: It denotes the state of being organized and also the groups that do the organizing. Typical organizations are hierarchical with a distinct and clear chain of command, which has meant that specific systems of management preserve the structures of these organizations. The hierarchical organization was robust because forming competing large institutional groups was relatively hard. Now, however, forming a group or alliance online is relatively easy. "Groups of people are complex, in ways that make those groups hard to form and hard to sustain," he argues. "Much of the shape of traditional institutions is a response to those difficulties. New social tools relieve some of those burdens, allowing for new kinds of group-forming, like using simple sharing to anchor the creation of new groups."[16]

Yochai Benkler also sees networks as both a collection of individual actions and as an underlying structure: "we can think of individuals as discrete entities in multiple intersecting networks, but also of organizations, or even techno-organizational forms, like WikiLeaks, as opposed to Julian Assange as the operative entity." To this effect, network power "describes the extent to which one entity in a network can affect the behavior, configurations, or outcomes of another entity, as well as the modality through which it can do so."[17] To Benkler, power within a network is the extent to which a node can influence other nodes in their behavior, outcomes, or configuration. In a related manner, freedom in a network is the extent to which individuals or entities can determine their own behavior.

Twenty years ago only mainstream media could have disseminated a video of the US helicopter attack on journalists in Iraq, as WikiLeaks did. Effective distribution would have depended on a small number of large-scale media outlets. Instead, WikiLeaks posted the video on a series of mirrored websites and it went viral in hours, ensuring its widespread global dissemination before governments had even had a chance to respond. In the networked society, power can be exercised through new channels.[18]

———

Political scientist and public policy leader Anne-Marie Slaughter has been influential in applying network theory to the international domain through the articulation of the idea of network power. While she ultimately argues that all major elements of society are networked—war (organization between different terrorist groups), diplomacy (intergovernmental cooperation), business (economic groups), media (interactive journalism), social relations (social networks)—she places much of her focus on the role of the state in these systems. She concludes, as we will see, that in the end, "Hierarchy and control lose out to community, collaboration, and self-organization."[19] Even in the heavily institutional world of global trade, networks have become the central organizing feature of markets. Global production networks, not nation-states, dominate the most dynamic structures of the economy.[20] Networks challenge the very existence and viability of hierarchical structures.

For Slaughter, power in networks lies in the ability to exert soft power: in networks, authority cannot be enforced—it needs to be acquired through endearment and obligation.[21] The power that flows from connectivity, she argues, is not the power to impose outcomes since "networks are not directed and controlled as much as they are managed and orchestrated . . . and multiple players are integrated into a whole that is greater than the sum of its parts."[22] Networked power instead flows from the ability to make a maximum number of valuable connections that strive toward some common political, economic, or social purpose.

According to Slaughter, global networks have fundamentally challenged the notion of Westphalian sovereignty first because these nation-states are simply not as effective in exerting power as they used to be. As Political Scientist Robert Keohane said in 1993, "It is now a platitude that the ability of governments to attain their objectives through individual action has been undermined by international political and economic interdependence." This, according to Slaughter, has been magnified by networked actors.[23]

Second, the Westphalian notion of absolute sovereignty is declining. The idea whereby the state has complete control of its territory and the welfare of its citizens is being challenged by any number of international legal regimes and norms, most notably the idea of the Responsibility to Protect, whereby a state's sovereignty is conditional on the protection of its citizens.

Following this qualification, Slaughter argues that there is a need for a different conceptualization of sovereignty, one that focuses on a state's capacity to participate in trans-governmental regimes and international institutions; this notion of sovereignty is inextricably linked to the existence of "government networks" operating across borders and the power that they wield.

The idea of "sovereignty as responsibility" also flows from this notion of evolving sovereignty. According to Slaughter, "The best illustration of the new sovereignty can be found in the operation of 'government networks'—networks of national government officials of all kinds operating across borders to regulate individuals and corporations operating in a global economy, combat global crime, and address common problems on a global scale." Slaughter argues that networked sovereignty is built on trust and relationships between participants, the exchange of information on a regular basis, collaboration on common issues, and the offer of technical assistance and professional socialization to members from less developed countries.

This definition of sovereignty relies almost entirely on the norms of state behavior. It includes many of the lessons of network theory and applies them to networks of states. However, there is a world of other actors participating in networks that overlap and intersect with state interests. What's more, these actors are not constrained by the same legal, ethical, and regulatory norms as states. And their objectives and goals need not be based in either personal or collective interests. Perhaps most important, they are very difficult to control.

Slaughter's argument for networked power, like Nye's soft power before it, ultimately privileges the state in the international system. They both recognize that hierarchies are threatened by networks, that new groups have power and influence, and that states need to adapt to remain relevant. This in itself is a remarkable shift in thinking. In a matter of a decade or two, a system of state-based power that has held for half a millennium is in the middle of a rapid transformation.

Ultimately, however, the network power and network sovereignty arguments fail to take the logic that underpins them to their conclusion. At their core, they are still about the state. They focus on how the state should and must adapt to remain relevant in this new world. But it could equally be true that the attributes that empower individuals and groups to challenge dominant actors are powerful enough to fundamentally threaten the viability of the state as a social construct. This is a far more radical proposition, and one with vast consequence. It poses a existential challenge to the viability of the state in a networked system, one that could signal a revolutionary break from the slow evolutionary history of the state system described earlier.

To me, the empowerment of digital actors raises fundamental questions for the international system. What are the implications that significant state responsibilities will be undermined or replaced by networked actors? Are the ethical and legal norms that we have embedded into our traditional institutions transferable to a networked world? What are the risks that our global security and economic institutions will be rendered obsolete or irrelevant? How are states fighting back, and are their actions stemming the tide or ultimately hastening their decline? And perhaps most important, how do we as a society engage those who have power now, rather than with those that once did?

To answer these questions, we have to first look in more detail at what gives networked actors power.

———

How has Anonymous, a seemingly disorganized, leaderless, diffuse group of digital activists, been able to take on the world's most powerful states and corporations? The answer gives us a window into the new world of disruptive power.

Information technology has radically lowered the barrier for entry into international collective action. As legal scholar Marvin Ammori argues, the marginal production and distribution costs are now so low that online participants are able to overcome the technological and logistical costs, and organizational barriers, to coordinated political action. This ability for ad hoc collaboration enables a network of individual participants driven by non-monetary motivations and leverages their excess labor capacity.[24]

A divide remains between who has access to this empowering technology and who doesn't. Ultimately, it is not simply about access (though access remains an issue) but about what people are able to do with that access. Most of our technology is designed by the affluent, for the affluent, which leads to a real bias in who is empowered by it. Disruptive power also privileges certain forms of knowledge. Knowing code, being comfortable with multiple identities, being curious and creative are powerful in the digital world.

The very qualities that give emergent actors their power run counter to the traditional norms of international power. What once made states weak—a lack of structure, instability, decentralized governance, loose and evolving ties—are precisely what makes groups like Anonymous powerful. Their alternative approach, which is rooted in the structures of contemporary information technology, is transforming the world of international affairs. This represents a revolution rather than an evolution in power and in this paradox lies the threat faced by the nation-state. And through an analysis of what makes Anonymous powerful we can identify the three core attributes of disruptive power—it is formless, unstable, and collaborative.

ONE: FORMLESS

You can't join Anonymous because it is not an organization. You can't lead it because there is no leader. You quit Anonymous by no longer participating. Because there is no centralized leadership, there are no gatekeepers. There is no one to decide on membership or to bestow "official status" on the organization. Most participants engage under a cloak of encryption and pseudonyms.

As one Anonymous participant put it, "Anonymous is not a club, a party or even a movement. There is no charter, no manifesto, no membership fees. Anonymous has no leaders, no gurus, no ideologists. In fact, it does not even have a fixed ideology."

This runs in direct contrast to the firm hierarchical structures that give traditional institutions strength. Think the United Nations, Ford Motor Company, the US military, the Red Cross. All gain power through the way they are ordered.

So how are we to understand an actor with a large amount of power but no institutional structure? The answer lies in the power that is gained because of, rather than in spite of, its decentralized and non-hierarchical nature—its formlessness. Anonymous, like the many other groups that are outlined in this book, is organized as a network. Existing primarily on an information network, Anonymous defies political, economic, and structural boundaries that encumber traditional institutions.

The inherent value of anonymity helps to explain the growing power of the individual in an online network. It is a technologically determined anonymity that allows individual users to engage in political speech without fear of retribution, and as such, gives them power.[25]

Communication within a network is highly decentralized. Planning and coordination for disparate activities can occur on any number of platforms. When any location or form of communication is compromised, a discussion simply moves on. This enables very rapid evolution and growth.

But hierarchies were created to maintain and legitimize sources of power—to be able to trace the information decision makers act on and ultimately to hold them to account. How do we replace these norms of accountability in a system with no clear power structure? Anonymous can't control who acts in its name, which can lead to inconsistencies. A pro-life hacker associated with Anonymous recently attacked Britain's largest abortion provider in 2011. Months later another Anonymous hacker attacked the Vatican for being pro-life. A recent white paper by the Internet security company McAfee concluded, "If hacktivists remain unfocused and continue to accept anyone who signs on to act on their behalf, we may be on the verge of a digital civil war."

Whether a radically decentralized organizational structure can be made accountable to its constituents or to society remains one of the most pressing questions surrounding disruptive power. A lack of rigid structure also makes groups like Anonymous remarkably resilient. After the arrests of the five top Anonymous hackers, attacks continued unabated. Because of the numerous paths that connect any two points, when one path is disabled, the network finds another and its effectiveness is not compromised.

Computer scientists have long studied the resilience of networks. A recent article in *Nature*, however, argues that not all redundant networks are equal. The authors show that one attribute of scale-free networks, such as the Internet, is that most of the network's nodes have one or two links; few nodes have more. This guarantees that the system is entirely connected and is therefore particularly robust. More specifically, nodes' ability to communicate with one another in networks such as the Internet is unaffected by high failure rates. This high tolerance for error comes at a price, however: if key nodes are attacked, the entire network becomes vulnerable.[26]

The Internet's resilience follows not only from its high tolerance for error but also from packet-switching. Cyber law scholar Michael Froomkin describes packet-switching as the method by which data can be broken up into standardized packets, which are then routed to their destinations via an indeterminate number of intermediaries.[27] Having many possible routes for communication means that information can still be transmitted when one break occurs. This is one reason the US Department of Defense developed the Internet.

And much like the Internet itself, networked actors are loosely connected, with very few people holding large numbers of the connections. This makes them incredibly hard to shut down and proves immensely frustrating for the traditional institutions they are disrupting.

TWO: UNSTABLE

In a digital network, information is both abundant and evolving at an increasingly fast pace. News of world events has become a commodity, and the evolution of ideas, ideologies, beliefs, and politics is happening almost in real time. Software programs, group behavior, and individual action are all adapting to a world of massive real-time data flows and what is amounting to a new pace of evolution. Groups like Anonymous thrive in this instability and uncertainty and can take advantage of the traditional actors who require predictable knowledge of the future to remain powerful.

Whether it concerns a corporation's knowledge of a market or a state's intelligence service, large 20th-century institutions expect a degree of predictability that is increasingly difficult to attain. This is in part due to the scale of data now being produced. For example, every five minutes we produce enough data to fill a Library of Congress. Much of this is tagged with a host of spatial and reference information and is social; two billion pieces of content are tagged by location each month on the Facebook platform alone. This flow of data is leading to a new law of production, where the more we consume, produce, and use data, the cheaper it becomes. Data is not subject to resource constraints.

The production of new information is outpacing our capability to understand it as a collective. This environment privileges actors who thrive on uncertainty and confusion, and cripples those that need long-term strategic planning to mobilize resources and implement policies.

This scale and pace of information production is leading to changes in how individuals behave. As one implication of this, in online networks, relationships are less likely to be grounded in history. Hence, group loyalty does not ensure path dependency. Often, a movement or campaign will create no permanent institution.

In this space, ideas can take on a life of their own, acting like viruses and self-marketing. In this way, messages act like "memes"—viral ideas that use people to replicate themselves.[28]

The flip side to rapid, viral distribution is that it privileges certain types of information. Internet theorist Evgeny Morozov warns that online networks, and the pace of change they enable, lead to a motivation to engage in superficial forms of politics, where individuals are incentivized to behave loudly and assertively.[29] If Morozov is right about the type of behavior that is disproportionately incentivized, then content that goes viral can be problematic. The Kony 2012 viral video, for example, was disruptive in that it managed to promote a cause that was absent from mainstream discourse and affect policy makers in a way traditional organizations had failed to, but it was ultimately flawed. Even so, its disruptive power, to both the traditional aid organizations and to the governments tasked with finding Joseph Kony, were clear.

THREE: COLLABORATIVE

We are so used to equating organization with hierarchy that it at first seems surprising that disparate groups can act collectively. In the international system, a state is defined as sovereign by an international organization like the United Nations. In a networked model, new actors require no outside party to attain status. Instead, their identities derive from what they do and from the impact they have. But if the Internet technologically empowers individuals to act on their own, how does it regulate collective behavior?

New forms of ad hoc governance are emerging in the networked environment. One idea is that there is an emerging form of self-regulation, that technology is enabling a new form of collective ad hoc private regulation whereby private actors deliberately constrain and influence other private actors.[30]

Harvard Law professor Lawrence Lessig, a leader in the global information technology debate, also argues that the legal control of behaviors is just one of many forms of constraints, including norms, markets, and system architecture. So the fact that a network is largely lawless does not mean that it is unregulated; it simply means that it is regulated by alternative (private) means.[31]

In 2002, Yochai Benkler adapted this idea of self-regulation to the Internet age. Benkler builds on the theory of Robert Coase, which classified the regulation of interactions as either market-based (via contracts) or hierarchy-based (via institutions), to posit that the Internet permits a third model of production: ad hoc volunteerism.[32]

In this governance system, credibility and authority are gained through action. In a lovely turn of phrase, Jenny Sundén says that on the Internet one "types oneself into being."[33] Similarly, Manuel Castells argues that the new actors gain their power from communication, not from representation.[34] Both imply that authority in online networks such as Anonymous is judged only by the reality the participants create.

Collaborative action has proven to be a critical attribute of disruptive innovators in international affairs. When Anonymous coordinates a distributed denial-of-service (DDoS) attack, hundreds or even thousands of computers act as a coordinated mob, overloading the servers of the target.

States and corporations collaborate, but in a formalized top-down manner, through negotiated treaties or mergers. While the concept of soft power would dictate that more informal influence is increasingly important, these approaches are intended to increase the power of the state.

They are not an end in themselves and they do not benefit all participants equally.

Anonymous, on the other hand, is an intrinsically social world based on partnerships, collaborations, and interdependencies. This stands in direct contrast to command-and-control hierarchies, market exchanges, and traditional bureaucratic instruments.

In the field of international relations the determinative effects of social behavior are intimately associated with the theory of constructivism, which posits that international dynamics are historically and socially constructed rather than purely a function of either human nature or state power.[35] In the online environment, many of the same dynamics are at work. danah boyd argues that MySpace and Facebook allow US youth to socialize with friends even when they are unable to gather in unmediated situations, thus serving the function of "networked publics" that support sociability.[36] Professor of Library, Archival and Information Studies Caroline Haythornthwaite argues that because individuals can articulate and make visible their social networks, individuals with "latent ties" can make connections that would not usually be made.[37] Clay Shirky goes a step further, arguing that peer-to-peer is "erasing the distinction between consumer and provider" and creating new forms of socioeconomic relationships.[38]

It is these social connections, intrinsic to an online network, that give it power. Logically, a group in which people can get to know many others and build genuine interpersonal connections will be stronger than one with very loose ties. These social connections are valuable to corporations and governments who want to know more about it, but they also give tremendous power back to the engaged public. Even groups with only latent ties allow connections to be made and people to be mobilized.

Because these networks are enabled by information technology, they also have a different relationship to space. The decentralized nodes of Anonymous, for example, are not geographically predicated. Still there is certainly segregation online. It is not based on geography, but generally on other factors like nationality, wealth, age, and level of education.

More important, groups like Anonymous show that collective action is possible without centralization and a hierarchical structure. Clay Shirky argues that collective activities that formerly required coordination and hierarchy can now be carried out through looser forms of coordination, such as social network connections, common short-term alignment in a movement, or unified objectives in a particular event. In this way, the Internet unites groups so disparate that they could not have been formed without it.[39]

Collective online action also enables groups previously marginalized by the threat of violence, such as those in autocratic states, to overcome what was a real collective action problem. Instead of having to risk death in the streets, movements can evolve in safer virtual environments. This virtual space has also become the location of real state oppression, which is explored throughout this book.

It is also potentially problematic that much of this online activity takes place on platforms owned by private corporations. Writing about networked governance, Mark Considine argues that a network is a social world based on partnerships, collaborations, and inter-dependencies, as opposed to command-and-control hierarchies, market exchange, and traditional bureaucratic instruments.[40] Manuel Castells adds that networks enable a new collective capitalism, the "signature form of organization in the information age."[41]

In the end, the relationship between public and private spaces is getting increasingly blurred, and states are regularly seeking private data from the companies that control the online space. YouTube, for example, has a policy against graphic videos but will make exceptions in the case of content that is important for human rights, such as violence against protestors in Bahrain in 2011. However, YouTube decides what is politically important.

What then are hierarchical institutions, such as states and corporations, to do in this new world? How are the traditional institutions that have long governed, controlled, and led (for good and ill) the international system going to adapt to these new actors? How can states engage in a world where the core tenets of their power have been flipped upside down?

In the following chapters, I explore this tension; show which actors are leveraging technology to solve problems, cease control, or take power; and how the legacy institutions are, and are not, fighting back.

CHAPTER THREE

SPACES OF DISSENT

On January 28, 2011, in the middle of a popular uprising against Egyptian president Hosni Mubarak that was organized on the Internet and amplified using social media, the Mubarak regime turned off most digital communications in Egypt. This striking display of state power served as a reminder that the free and open communications enabled by digital technology remain susceptible to state control.

Members of Telecomix, a decentralized network of mostly Western hackers and activists committed to freedom of expression, saw Mubarak's Internet blockage as an outrageous restriction of a basic human freedom. They began figuring out how to reestablish network connections in Egypt.

When the Internet wasn't entirely shut down, Telecomix members provided Egyptian activists with surveillance-circumvention tools such as Tor, which anonymizes digital communications, and virtual private networks. They built mirrors and proxies to restore access to blocked websites. Using a network tool called nMap, they scanned the entire Egyptian Internet Protocol (IP) address space to find a few thousand machines that still had access to the Internet and injected human-readable messages into their web-server logs describing how to engage online safely and securely.

They manually relayed tweets from Egyptians without access to Twitter via Internet relay chatrooms (IRCs).

When Egyptian Internet and mobile service was fully shut down, Telecomix partnered with the French Data Network, a hacker-friendly Internet service provider, to set up hundreds of dial-up modem lines. They also worked with amateur radio enthusiasts to send short logistical messages over designated frequencies. To let Egyptian activists know about these alternate services, Telecomix found as many fax lines as they could in Egypt. The international group sent out thousands of leaflets to fax machines at university campuses, cybercafes, and businesses explaining how to get around the blackouts, as well as medical information about such topics as how to treat someone exposed to tear gas. They also set up fax machines to transmit news out of Egypt. "When countries block, we devolve," Telecomix member Peter Fein said.

Telecomix originally came together in Sweden in April 2009 in response to a proposed European Union (EU) law that would to cut off Internet access to anyone who repeatedly downloaded copyrighted files. They believed such legislation would restrict the free flow of information over the Internet. Before a vote could take place, the group published the phone numbers of every EU Parliament member, then enlisted the Pirate Bay, a file-sharing website that attracted 20 million monthly visitors at the time, to link to them. European parliament phones were jammed for several days, and legislators subsequently dropped the proposed statute.

After this first, successful campaign, international participation in Telecomix quickly grew. While united by a general commitment to "keeping the Internet running," there was no singular leadership or direction. "Think of Telecomix as an ever growing bunch of friends that do things together," the founder, Chris Kullenberg told journalist Andy Greenberg. On its website Telecomix states that they "know no borders technological or territorial. We have no specific agenda, IRCocratic leadership and no pre-determined practices. We are an occurrence rather than a group."[1]

Peter Fein, who emerged as somewhat of a spokesperson for the group, wrote on his blog, "Telecomix is an ad hoc disorganization of Internauts who support free communication for everyone, regardless of political affiliation. Comprised of programmers, punks, politicians, pirates, and others, Telecomix believes in person-to-person communication— the original p2p." These people are "motivated by radical passion for freedom" and "drawn together by the desire to have an Internet adventure, to see what free communication can do in the lives of ordinary people."[2]

As Telecomix worked in support of Egyptian activists, its Internet Relay Chatrooms (IRC) became information technology (IT) support centers for other activists and revolutionaries. As conflict began in Syria, Telecomix agents in France, Germany, and Sweden disseminated videos and photographs of atrocities committed by Assad's police and military forces. Telecomix anticipated an Internet shutdown in Syria similar to what happened in Egypt. Instead, the Assad regime monitored Internet and social-media activity of rebel groups and activists.

For Telecomix, this approach posed a new challenge: how to send messages without identifying the activists they sought to help and putting their lives in danger. A Telecomix agent who goes by the screen name of KheOps wrote that this concern ruled out Facebook, which the Syrian government was monitoring.[3] So the group tried a brute-force solution. Members crawled the web for as many Syrian email addresses as they could collect—including addresses for pro-Assad groups and individuals—and sent the following message:

Dear People of Syria. Fighters for democracy

This is Telecomix. Hacktivists fighting for the flow of information.

Please find attached guidelines that should help you communicate safely and broadcast information. Please read it carefully. Spread it as much as you can, by any means. Democracy, freedom are at stake. We struggled to make this message reach you because of censorship.

With freedom feelings.

With kind regards.

Telecomix

Telecomix didn't really know how many of the people they were trying to help had received the messages. As KheOps explains, it was "as if we had sent thousands of carrier-pigeons over the border, we did not get any direct feedback. . . . Our involvement and concern had increased a lot, but the other side of the wall still seemed terribly silent. We thus took a step towards a more penetrating action."[4]

Telecomix also built a simple website that included Internet security guidelines in Arabic and a small downloadable software package containing Firefox browser plugins, a Tor bundle, secure instant-messaging software, and a link to the Telecomix IRC. The group used 19 mirror sites with different domains to avoid being blocked. KheOps called the successful initiative a combination of "high technical skills, deep emotional involvement and decentralized technological power."

Members of Telecomix also scanned the Syrian Internet in search of devices vulnerable to hacking. They acquired user passwords and got into Cisco Systems-produced network switches, cameras streaming live street scenes, and computers of Syrian government officials. They found 5,000 unsecured home routers and warned their owners about their vulnerability to state surveillance.[5] A Telecomix member known by the screen name Punkbob discovered logs showing the Internet activity of thousands of Syrians including their locations, the sites they visited, and the complete contents of their communications. The logs came from a device built by Blue Coat Systems. Punkbob, who claims to be a Pentagon contractor, recognized them because, he said, the Pentagon uses the same software to filter and track the Internet use of its employees. The Syrian government was spying on its citizens using US-made devices. Telecomix made this data public, spurring widespread public scrutiny of Blue Coat Systems and similar Western surveillance device manufacturers and playing a role in a US executive order against the export of such technology to Syria and Iran.

Telecomix does not fit comfortably in our traditional categories of participants in international affairs. It is not a nation-state, a formal institution, or a rogue individual. It has a collective identity and its loose, decentralized structure makes it difficult to control.

"If Telecomix exists anywhere, it's in our chat networks and the relationships of the people who participate. We operate on a simple principle: you show up, find collaborators, and just go do," Peter Fein said in a 2012 talk at the Personal Democracy Forum conference. "Like the rest of the Internet, Telecomix is put together with bubble gum and popsicle sticks—some days the server crashes, or gets DDoS'd or someone forgets to pay the domain bill and nothing seems to ever get written down. This turns out to be a good thing, because when the Internet breaks, we can get some more popsicle sticks and go fix it."[6]

This allows for a legal, organizational, practical, and technical fluidity that traditional institutions do not enjoy. Fein continues, "When the net went down in Egypt, Telecomix didn't call Ron Wyden to call Hillary Clinton to call Obama to call Mubarak and say, 'please turn the Internet back on.' Instead we took direct action—we got out some modems and faxes and just did it ourselves."

Groups like Telecomix and Anonymous represent a new kind of international actor that is remaking international affairs. The two movements may employ different tactics; in Tunisia, where the Arab Spring began, Anonymous took down the websites of the prime minster and the government while Telecomix distributed encryption technology to protestors. But they are both groups of hackers, and their members act at great personal risk because of a shared ethical belief that freedom of information is a universal right. In his 1984 work on hackers, Steven Levy argues that hackers are bound to two principles: First, they fight corporate control of the Internet and work to remove the barriers that allow corporations to control information and behavior online. Second, they believe that centralization of power—especially the power of the state—has led to wide abuse and needs to be challenged.[7] This, of course, is a form of anarchism. Instead of manifesting as violence or protest, however, groups like Telecomix seek to illustrate the deficiency of state power by demonstrating their own decentralized capabilities.

———

For groups like Telecomix, hacking is a form of civil disobedience. Henry David Thoreau coined the term in his 1849 essay titled *Civil Disobedience*, which drew on his opposition to slavery and the Mexican-American War. To Thoreau, governments exist because people have assigned them representation and they should not take obedience to the state for granted. States needed to earn the loyalty of their citizens by pursuing justice and conscientiousness. In the absence of such virtues, he argued, civil disobedience is not only natural but should be encouraged. Civil disobedience was a check on state power. Thoreau was not an anarchist, but he did believe "that government is best which governs the least," and that "government, at its best, is an expedient." He believed that each individual needs to listen to his or her conscience and question the rule of the government and its institutions, even at the cost of destabilizing "the collective" and ending in loss of government.

Thoreau's position was a radical one, and others have followed his line of thinking. In *A Theory of Justice*, John Rawls defines civil disobedience as "a public, non-violent and conscientious breach of law undertaken with the aim of bringing about a change in laws or government policies." This act needed to be conscientious, with a sincere moral conviction and the greater good of society in mind. It needed a political motivation, appealing to a "common conception of justice." It had to be aimed at changing the law to bring it into conformity with justice. It needed to be nonviolent, and participants had to accept any punishment that might result from their actions.

Hannah Arendt added a measure of populism to these definitions, seeing civil disobedience as representative of a groundswell of public dissent that emerges when enough people believe that action is needed outside the formal mechanisms for changing or informing government policy.[8] She wrote this before the rise of the Internet, which facilitates mass expression with less friction or commitment than a physical protest.[9]

In the 1950s, students at MIT coined the term "hacking" to refer to pranks played in early artificial intelligence labs and experiments with track circuitry by the Tech Model Railroad Club.[10] Journalist Quinn Norton, who has covered the hacking world for a decade, defines it as "clever misuse of any technology."[11] While not explicitly a form of civil disobedience, it has always had an anti-authoritarian undercurrent. In a 1986 article titled "The Conscience of a Hacker," a hacker calling himself the Mentor wrote:

> We explore . . . and you call us criminals. We seek after knowledge . . . and you call us criminals. . . . You build atomic bombs, you wage wars, you murder, cheat, and lie to us and try to make us believe it's for our own good, yet we're the criminals. Yes, I am a criminal. My crime is that of curiosity. My crime is that of judging people by what they say and think, not what they look like. My crime is that of outsmarting you, something that you will never forgive me for. I am a hacker, and this is my manifesto. You may stop this individual, but you can't stop us all.[12]

The first commonly recognized instance of hacking as a form of political activism came in October 1989. An antinuclear worm called WANK (Worms against Nuclear Killers) placed a message on login screens at the National Aeronautics and Space Administration (NASA) and the US Energy Department that said, "WORMS AGAINST NUCLEAR KILLERS . . . Your System Has Been Officially WANKed." The first distributed denial-of-service (DDoS) attack, which overwhelms a website or server with communication requests, was an act of civil disobedience. In 1994, an activist group known as Zippies "email bombed" US government websites in protest of a law banning outdoor raves.

In 1996, a collective of media professionals and artists calling themselves the Critical Art Ensemble released a manifesto of sorts called "Electronic Civil Disobedience and Other Unpopular Ideas."[13] They argued that information flows electronically, not through castles and city centers, and consequently, the mode of opposition to power had to change. In 1998, a group called the Electronic Disturbance Theater (EDT) began what they called acts of electronic civil disobedience against the Mexican government in support of the Zapatistas, a leftist rural movement in the southern state of Chiapas. The Zapatista campaign inspired other movements. In 1998, the EDT launched FloodNet—a software that could enable DDoS attacks. Part protest, part digital performance art, the idea behind the project, as explained by cofounder Brett Stalbaum, was to serve as "conceptual net art that empowers people through activist and artistic expression." In 1999, the worlds of physical and electronic activism merged with the World Trade Organization (WTO) protests, where a new round of international trade liberalization negotiations were being launched. While protesters rallied in the streets of Seattle, a group called the Electrohippies Collective, based in Oxford, England, mobilized 450,000 people to participate in a DDoS attack on the WTO website.

Academic Molly Sauter sees these and subsequent acts of electronic activism as a new form of civil disobedience. "Networked technologies mean our opportunities for effective political activism have increased exponentially. Where activists once put their physical bodies on the line to fight for their causes, online activists can engage in digitally-based acts of civil disobedience from their keyboards."[14] Sauter identifies three types of online civil disobedience: using direct disruption tactics such as DDoS attacks and website defacements; ferreting out hidden or secret information; and providing activists with additional information channels. Together, "these tactics aim to upset the status quo by disrupting the normal flow of information, thereby attracting attention to their [the activists'] cause and message." And digital civil disobedience is dynamic, she wrote. "The future of digital civil disobedience will grow out of new online tactics, augmented by the Internet's ability to bring people together across geographical boundaries."[15]

Like acts of offline civil disobedience, digital efforts are ethically motivated, reject violence, a profit motive, and destruction of property; and participants accept personal responsibility for their actions. Yet the terrain is much less clear.[16] The word "disobedience" implies that laws are broken, but law has been slow to adapt to the digital realm. As for the "civil" part, disobedience online frequently crosses jurisdictional boundaries, and its targets can include any entity that is perceived to have power. The motivation for an act of civil disobedience online is not always apparent, as protesters can act anonymously, motivated by everything from political conviction to fun. And what does it mean to be violent or destructive online? Is a DDoS attack an act of speech or more akin to smashing a window?

With these and other early displays of online political activism, governments and security strategists anticipated a potential threat. This range of digitally enabled activist behavior poses a real challenge for policy- and lawmakers. In 2001, two Rand Corporation analysts, David Ronfeldt and John Arquilla, defined what they called Netwar as an "emerging mode of conflict (and crime) at societal levels, short of traditional military warfare, in which the protagonists use network forms of organization and related doctrines, strategies, and technologies attuned to the information age. These protagonists," they argue, "are likely to consist of dispersed organizations, small groups, and individuals who communicate, coordinate, and conduct their campaigns in an internetted manner, often without a central command."[17]

Reflecting on what the rise of Netwar meant for the state, Ronfeldt and Arquilla came to two particularly prescient conclusions. First, they argued, Netwar has both dystopian and benign manifestations. Some, such as terrorist groups, may prove a threat to the state. Others, such as NGOs, civil society groups, and liberation movements, might have perceived beneficial effects. Both, however, use similar tools and tactics. This dual nature, or "ambivalence" as they describe it, is challenging for the state to engage with.

Second, they argued that networks are very hard to counter with hierarchical organizations. They warn that "governments tend to be so constrained by hierarchical habits and institutional interests that it may take some sharp reverses—such as were just suffered in the terrorist attacks in the United States—before a willingness to experiment more seriously with networking emerges."[18] Ronfeldt and Arquilla wrote this article in the months before the September 11, 2001, terrorist attacks on the United States, and as will be explored throughout this book, these attacks provided the regulatory and legal justification for the US government to experiment as a networked rather than a hierarchical actor.

Cyberactivism has reached critical mass with the proliferation of groups like Anonymous. Given their influence and the scale of their operations, it is almost impossible to ignore their role in civil society. But the tension between hacking as activism and hacking as terrorism has long been present.

In testimony before the House Armed Services Committee in 2000, information security researcher Dorothy Denning reflected on the impact of the electrohippies' DDoS protest on the World Trade Organization in 1999. How should this act be interpreted by the state?

> To the best of my knowledge, no attack so far has led to violence or injury to persons, although some may have intimidated their victims. Both the EDT and the electrohippies view their operations as acts of civil disobedience, analogous to street protests and physical sit-ins, not as acts of violence or terrorism. This is an important distinction. Most activists, whether participating in the Million Moms March or a Web sit-in, are not terrorists. My personal view is that the threat of cyberterrorism has been mainly theoretical, but it is something to watch and take reasonable precautions against.[19]

The attacks of 9/11 and other events rendered such nuanced thinking moot in US political discourse. In February 2012, the US National Security Agency (NSA) labeled Anonymous a threat to national security, claiming they "could have the ability within the next year or two to bring about a limited power outage through a cyber attack."[20]

———

Anonymous is a leaderless organization that is horizontal, decentralized, and all-inclusive. Some argue that it is not even an organization but an umbrella brand under which individuals sharing the same ideology come together to carry on activities of online activism. Nevertheless, the United States, the United Kingdom, and other governments have charged individuals suspected of being connected to Anonymous with crimes. In March 2012, the FBI arrested Jeremy Hammond for hacking into the private intelligence firm Stratfor and stealing the personal details of more than 850,000 people (published by WikiLeaks as the "Global Intelligence Files"). That September, Barrett Brown, the self-proclaimed spokesperson for Anonymous, was indicted on 17 counts including conspiracy, corruption, concealing evidence, and violating the Computer Fraud and Abuse Act.

The zeal in making examples of actions associated with Anonymous is alarming. "Those who have the skills and capacity to electronically enter these closed systems of information terrify the state," Chris Hedges reflected during Hammond's trial. "And the state, when it confronts those who have this capacity, uses everything at its disposal to destroy these opponents."[21] Most of them are young adults with no prior criminal records, yet they are being treated like career criminals. They have been pressured into turning against one another and imprisoned long before they were sentenced. Their families have also become targets; Barrett Brown's mother has been forced to plead guilty to charges relating to hiding her son's laptop from the Federal Bureau of Investigation (FBI) and now could face a fine of $100,000 and up to one year in jail or six months of probation. Brown's attorney, Jay Leiderman, thinks the FBI intends to send a message through these and other first-generation computer fraud cases: "The government is saying loud and clear, if you use computers in ways that make us feel uncomfortable you go to jail and you go to jail for a very, very long time."[22]

The government also seems to be making an example of Chelsea Manning, a former US military private first class who was arrested for releasing to WikiLeaks more than 250,000 US diplomatic cables, 400,000 US Army Reports about Iraq, 90,000 US Army Reports about Afghanistan, many other classified US government documents, and the video of a Baghdad airstrike that killed civilians. Manning's stated motivation for the leak was to "expose the American military's 'bloodlust' and disregard for human life in Iraq and Afghanistan."[23] Initially Manning was charged on 12 counts, all based on leaking unauthorized and classified materials. In March 2011, the charges were modified; this time she was charged on 22 counts, including aiding the enemy (which potentially carries the death penalty), wrongfully storing information, bypassing computer security, and adding unauthorized software. On February 28, 2013, she pled guilty to 10 out of 22 counts; she denied the most severe one, aiding and abetting the enemy, which rests on the notion that she knew that al-Qaeda had access to the Internet, and therefore gave them state secrets by posting them online.

By most accepted international definitions, Manning has been tortured by the US government. Since her arrest on May 29, 2010, she has been held in Iraq, Kuwait, Maryland, and finally in the military base in Quantico, Virginia, where she spent nine months in a six-by-eight-foot maximum-security cell. Manning was allowed out for 20 minutes a day, shackled, and deprived of almost all human contact. She was allowed to sleep only between 1 PM and 11 PM, naked and facing a bright light. Professor Juan Méndez, the UN Special Rapporteur on Torture and Other Cruel, Inhuman or Degrading Treatment or Punishment, accused the US government of treating Manning inhumanely.[24]

Manning was acquitted of aiding and abetting the enemy, a charge grounded in an 1863 case in which a Union soldier was charged with passing information to the South by talking to a newspaper reporter. Yet this zealous prosecution seems intended to establish new legal norms in dealing with hacking. As the *New York Times* reported, "Leakers are being prosecuted and punished like never before. Consider that the federal Espionage Act, passed in 1917, was used only three times in its first 92 years to prosecute government officials for press leaks. But the Obama administration, in the president's first term alone, used it six times to go after leakers. Now some of them have gone to jail."[25] In a March 2013 *New York Times* article titled "Death to Whistle-Blowers," Floyd Abrams and Yochai Benkler argued that "If successful, the prosecution will establish a chilling precedent: national security leaks may subject the leakers to a capital prosecution or at least life imprisonment. Anyone who holds freedom of the press dear should shudder at the threat that the prosecution's theory presents to journalists, their sources and the public that relies on them."[26] That did not happen, but given the current climate, journalists could be charged under the Espionage Act in the future. During the Manning trial, the judge asked the prosecution if they would "be going after Manning the same way if he had given the info to *NYT* or *Washington Post* instead of WikiLeaks?" They replied with a resounding yes.

———

Societies have a history of ostracizing protesters engaging in civil disobedience only to praise them later as foundational to the development of the culture. With digital activism, the state is seeking control in the only way it knows how: through the force of law and legal precedent. In so doing, however, it is not only radically redefining the enforcement tools at its disposal but also challenging unwritten social conventions about how to respond to civil disobedience. Spending a night in jail is different from serving a 30-year prison sentence, and this stricter response narrows the spaces of dissent that are fundamental to a democratic system, if not closing them off altogether. Political dissent, and the escape valve that it represents, requires a system in which just punishment is both proportional and known.

Dissent is a social escape valve, a check against the immense power we choose to give to the state, and there are costs to shutting it off. In her 1970 essay "Civil Disobedience," Hannah Arendt called civil disobedience a mechanism that sustains the democratic process by "interrupting the authority and sovereignty of the state." For Arendt, unchallenged sovereignty is the greatest threat to democracy because it "disintegrates plurality and the multiplicities within the space of appearance that are required for authentic political life." In this way, the coming together of the social collective is not "dissent"; it is the opposite since it demonstrates the "consent" of the citizens about issues they face.[27]

This view of civil disobedience as a collective act has roots in Jürgen Habermas, who saw it as a tool for deliberative democracy and a communicative action that was conducted in the public space. Actions in this public sphere can sit awkwardly between the laws that govern society and the laws being protested, but, he argues, "the right to civil disobedience remains suspended between legitimacy and legality for good reasons. But the constitutional state which prosecutes civil disobedience as a common crime falls under the spell of an authoritarian legalism."

In both offline and online formulations of civil disobedience there is a tension between the moral and ethical judgments of citizens and the legal constraints imposed on them by government. This puts public policymakers in a difficult position. They can accept a certain degree of dissent as healthy for a political system, but they must acknowledge that this implies a limitation of the law. Perhaps more challenging, they must make a qualitative distinction as to which dissenting behavior is tolerable or even healthy to politics and governance, and which behavior crosses a line that moves it into higher order criminality.

In zealously prosecuting activist hackers, the state is doing more than breaking its bargain with citizens. As Quinn Norton states, "Democracy was supposed to be different. It was supposed to be more flexible, not just for the benefit of the dissenters, but to keep the whole project from spiraling into the kind of craziness that caused empires and great nations to rot, fail, and fall from within. The rule of law became justice as it represented the needs of people, not just the majority, but of wisdom and progress—a balancing of thought and time." In this balance, "opposition was not only a right, but the only quality that kept power sane." It is this check on power that we are at risk of losing.

The state is in a bind, since the Internet is a far more difficult place to control than the public square, and acts of civil disobedience share form and tactics with more subversive and threatening behavior. Whether it is possible to control the Internet, the effort to do so could undermine the democratic state by intimidating its citizens and destroying its own character in the process.

CHAPTER FOUR

NEW MONEY

Ross William Ulbricht, a physics student in his late 20s from Austin, Texas, ran Silk Road, a hidden online market-place, from 2011 until his arrest by the FBI on October 2, 2013. He took over the site and the pseudonym Dread Pirate Roberts from its founder, who left for unknown reasons and remains at large.

"Silk Road is about freedom," Dread Pirate Roberts declared in his January 2012 State of the Road Address.[1] The goal is to "grow into a force to be reckoned with that can challenge the powers that be and at last give people the options to choose freedom over tyranny."

Silk Road wouldn't show up in a Google search. It could only be accessed using the encryption tool Tor, and it had many changing web addresses. Once shoppers arrived at the Silk Road, they could purchase a wide range of illicit goods including drugs, unregulated cigarettes, and forged documents. Much like Ebay, anyone could be a seller, and the product and services were ranked and reviewed by users. A drug order would be vacuum sealed and sent via the US postal service.

According to Carnegie Mellon researcher Nicolas Christin, the site grossed $1.2 million a month in the first half of 2012,[2] and an analyst at Dublin Trinity College found the site received 60,000 visits a day and had over a million active users.[3]

Essential to the site's viability, such as it was, was anonymity. And this is where money comes in. Traditionally black markets stay out of the reach of the state by using cash. The Silk Road, however, could exist online by using a new form of electronic currency called Bitcoin. And at the time, the Silk Road was the primary global market for the use of the currency, with sales of over nine and a half million Bitcoins, which at the time would have been worth over a billion dollars.[4]

To Dread Pirate Roberts, this was the true power of his venture. Silk Road was about citizens taking power (over currency and the free market) back from the state. "The people now can control the flow and distribution of information and the flow of money," he argued.[5] "Sector by sector the state is being cut out of the equation and power is being returned to the individual."

And as a person claiming to be a new Dread Pirate Roberts declared, "Silk Road is an idea, and where Silk Road now lies is in the people who made it what it was and it is those people who will, with a little help, bring the idea back to life again under a new name."[6]

And so is the case with the idea of Bitcoin. While many saw it as inextricably linked to illicit exchanges and therefore made less viable with the closing of the Silk Road, others see this as a watershed moment. Marco Santori, the chairman of the regulatory affairs committee of the Bitcoin Foundation, told the *New Yorker*'s Brian Patrick Eha, "Bitcoin's P.R. problem, with which it has struggled for the last year or so, is being addressed in a very direct way."[7]

Eha continues, "With the bugaboo of Silk Road banished, Bitcoin might soon acquire a relatively clean-cut image. That would allow cryptocurrency entrepreneurs to attract even more funding for companies built on what the Bitcoin Foundation considers the legitimate and valuable uses of Bitcoin—among them e-commerce, remittances, and financial empowerment for people in the Third World."[8]

While the Silk Road was an initial trial run for the nascent Bitcoin network, its closure by the FBI, which importantly did not exploit the currency's code, has ushered in a new era of development and hype.

Which takes us to a coffee shop in Vancouver, British Columbia, Canada.

———

Waves Coffee House is an ordinary-looking, Starbucks-like coffee shop in an upper-middle-class neighborhood of clean, comfortable Vancouver. In the back of the cafe, there is an automatic teller machine (ATM) that allows people to deposit cash in exchange for Bitcoins. In its first eight days of operation, the machine processed $81,000 Canadian dollars (CAD), and in its first month the ATM took in more than a million Canadian dollars.[9] Bitcoins purchased through the ATM are either deposited into an existing wallet or into a newly created one. Over half the transactions to date have been into new wallets. In other words, the machine is drawing new Bitcoin users. The system is run by a Canadian company called Robocoin, which plans to introduce the ATMs in locations across the country.

Where Robocoin leaves off (that is, once you have purchased Bitcoins), another Canadian company called Coinkite steps in. Coinkite allows you to connect your Bitcoin wallet to your debit card and provides debit-like machines for merchants so they can accept Bitcoins at the point of sale. As founder Jamie Robinson explains, "We're really trying to integrate Bitcoin into the mainstream."[10] A similar American company, Coinbase, has just received a $20 million investment from one of Silicon Valley's blue-chip venture funds. In spite of its black market past, Bitcoin is going mainstream.

Is any of this legal? It is not entirely clear. According to a 2013 report by the Canada Revenue Agency, the government views Bitcoins as virtual money and distinguishes them from a "traditional currency." This makes them a barter good that must be taxed.[11] Similarly, the US Department of Justice recently told a Senate committee that they consider Bitcoins and other digital currencies a "legal means of exchange."[12]

But these trepidatious state responses mask an underlying tension at the core of the Bitcoin movement. Is Bitcoin a commodity, whose value is very difficult to control and would therefore make adoption challenging? Or is it an emerging currency, which poses a real threat to the power states derive from their monopolies over currency control?

This is in many ways a debate for economists, one discussed later in the chapter, but it also represents markedly different political visions from proponents of the emerging technology—one seen in the transition from Silk Road to Coinbase. Whereas some see cryptocurrency as a radical anarchistic decoupling from the state, others (such as Silicon Valley investors) see it as a new financial mechanism, like Paypal.

In short, there is a growing divide in the Bitcoin community between crypto-anarchists who want to use Bitcoin as a libertarian weapon against the state and financial institutions, and the Silicon Valley venture capitalists who want to make Bitcoin a legal form of exchange by normalizing it within state control. Governments are stuck somewhere in the middle.

This chapter first outlines the history of the close connection between the control of currency and state power. It then details the rise of cryptocurrencies, explains how they work, and discusses their potential real-world benefits. Finally, it explores the potential challenge to state power, analyzes the critiques, and suggests possible futures.

While there is much debate as to the extent of Bitcoins' influence, as Alec Ross, a former senior adviser on innovation to Secretary of State Hillary Clinton, argues, "This phenomenon is part of a wider trend towards networked and globalized power structures that tend to undermine the nation-state-based systems to which we have grown accustomed."[13]

As such, it is critical that we understand it.

———

Whether it be through tax regimes, global trade systems, or reserve currency disputes, control of currency is an important attribute of state power. But it was not always thus. In fact, the connection between the money and state power has gone through several evolutions. It took centuries for currency to become the sole bastion of the state. If cryptocurrencies have the potential to destabilize this dynamic, then it is important to trace the evolution of money as a lever of state power.

As Benn Steil describes in *Money, Markets and Sovereignty*, for most of history, money has either literally been a metal (gold, silver, or copper) or been tied to the value of a commodity (the gold standard).[14] These metals were mined and traded in rough forms or primitive coins. When "coining," or the fashioning of standard coins from metal, became widespread in the ancient world, it gave people the ability to travel longer distances and to form wider trade and social networks. The first recorded instances of coins being "sealed" or stamped with a guarantee of weight and purity, were in the seventh century BC, starting with private sealing in the Mediterranean and then spreading to Asia.

With emerging political control over the manufacturing of coins came abuses in power. In one of the first examples of elites manipulating currency for their own benefit, kings in Lydia created monopolies on coining to control the amount of gold in the coins, often vastly reducing the gold content to profit off the discrepancy. Persian conquerors then helped to spread this style of coining to Asia and Northern Europe. Various kingdoms had their own coins, but it was the Romans in the third century BC who established a central currency system and delegitimized the use of any other type of coins. The Romans also systematically inflated the value of currency by reducing the gold content in their coins, causing political unrest.

Currency production as a lever of state power became entrenched around this period of history. The idea is that the state has a natural role in currency creation because it acts as a neutral body that can guarantee a currency's worth. Economist Robert Mundell, however, calls this a "textbook fiction" because, he argues, states were always motivated to control currency to reap potential profits rather than through any notion of establishing financial stability.[15]

As state control over money normalized, debates emerged over the authority and legitimacy of the state to control production, and over the efficiency of producing commodity-based currency on a mass scale. As Steil details, in the Renaissance period Charles Dumoulin was influential in arguing that money could have an "assigned value" apart from its specific value based on its metal composition. However, for this system to function, the "consent and usage of the people" was essential. Dumoulin did not believe that money should be completely separate from its commodity value—he called that notion "irrational and ridiculous"—but he saw how coins worth an agreed-upon amount could reduce legal disputes. In this same period, Italian mathematician Geminiano Montenari argued that individual states could create money when they saw fit, but if they were to trade with other nations, the worth of their currency had to meet a certain standard of gold or silver.

On the other side of the Atlantic, practical matters drove the evolution toward a national currency. Early US currency arose out of the need to standardize disparate currency systems, a hodgepodge of gold coins of varying purity and a wide range of foreign coins.[16] A centralized currency could be used to collect taxes and to bind together the colonies. The first colony to issue its own paper money was Massachusetts, in 1690. It was used to make loans to farmers, with the understanding that they could trade the money in on future tax collections. This gave the colonial powers more credibility as use of the currency grew without depreciation.

Slowly, then, the state was getting into the currency business. But as the scale of state influence over society grew, so too did the need to "anchor" the value of state-issued currency to a common norm. The Coinage Act of 1816 established the principle that state-issued paper could be tied to the value of gold, and could be converted into gold "on demand." This evolution was as much technology-driven as it was expedient. The technology used to mint these token coins (and make them counterfeit-proof) had not existed until this period, which is a key reason that the act was not passed until this time.

Gradually, more countries followed. Germany passed the gold standard in 1871, and the United States in 1873. But by then, the gold standard had served to consolidate British power, making the British the world's bankers and London the global financial center. Many foreign governments opened banks in London so that their transactions could easily be conducted in gold. Critically, Britain never actually made a commitment to following the gold standard. Instead, the public developed a trust that the banks and government would take action when required to inflate or deflate currency to protect them from shocks in value. Citizens saw a benefit to ceding control over currency valuation to political and financial institutions. The age of decentralized and disparate currencies was over.

Gold was not perfect and was still vulnerable to shocks—for example, substantial gold discoveries between 1849 and 1851 drove its value down. However, there has never been an alternative to gold that resulted in the same high levels of stability and international integration. Governments, in effect, relinquished an aspect of "sovereignty" in currency control in the hope of ensuring a stable economy. And it was this measure of stability that kept the gold standard in use well into the 20th century.

Though the financial system maintained stability throughout this period, several trends led to a shift away from the gold standard and toward government issued and controlled money—or, from fiduciary money, which can be converted to gold, to fiat money, which is convertible only into denominations of its own kind.

At the turn of the century, governments were holding vast amounts of gold in reserve and were increasingly tempted to put it to use. When they did put more of their gold into circulation, they could no longer promise that their currency could literally be exchanged for gold. Additionally, once governments had control over the production of bank notes, they could debase the currency for their own profit and use political and fiscal justifications for it without needing the consent of civilians. Governments faced pressures from exporters, debtors, and miners who benefited from the currency being debased or inflated. Shifting the determination of currency valuation from commodity value to the state led to abuse. "This is the fundamental conundrum facing a fiduciary money regime," argues Steil; "the better it works, the more compelling the logic for letting it slide towards a fiat regime." So, governments worldwide began using up the gold reserves and replacing them with US or British currency, which was also supposed to be backed by a percentage of gold reserves.

While some economists believe that the Great Depression would not have been such a widespread disaster if governments had not intervened by expanding credit, many others, including Fisher and Keynes, blamed the gold standard and saw economic sovereignty as the answer to the economic collapse. Such sovereignty would insulate a national economy from economic fluctuations and the chaos and unpredictability of the international markets.

By the middle of the 20th century, the Bretton Woods system had all but established the US dollar as the global standard. Foreign currencies could be converted to US dollars, and US dollars to gold. To keep this increasingly tenuous connection to the value of gold intact, the United States was required to hold only 25% of the value of its currency in gold, but by the 1960s the US gold supply had diminished to a point that the government could not uphold even this convertibility requirement, and in 1971, it "unbound" the US dollar from the gold standard completely.

And so began the age of currencies decoupled from a stable commodity value. Governments now had to fix their currency to their own reserves, either in their national currency or in US dollars. This had dual consequences: It made the control of currency and its value vulnerable to factors outside the purview of the state; at the same time it placed tremendous power in the hands of financial policymakers.

There is much debate, beyond the bounds of this book, over the wisdom and efficacy of nationally controlled currencies. What is undoubtable, however, is that they give governments tremendous power over the economies and livelihoods of their citizens. This is more often than not a good thing, and in democratic societies, there are means of giving authority and legitimacy to this power. But whether it be through the US financial crisis, the crash of the euro, national defaults in Greece and Argentina, or the increasingly volatile connection of national currencies to domestic resource markets, the credibility and capability of the state to control the value and stability of currencies, is, for some states, waning.

One need only look to the tumultuous history of the euro. In many ways, the euro was conceived on the very notion that control of currency was tied inextricably to power. The euro was seen not just as a means to normalize trade relations between European countries and to expand the overall European access to and integration with global markets, but also to legitimize the power of a common political system—the European Union—and to quite literally solidify the postwar peace.

In an article titled "Why the Euro Failed and How It Will Survive," Pedro Schwartz argues that the euro was designed to have an effect similar to that of the gold standard in that it would be very difficult to devalue but would still keep a measure of flexibility. It was based on the idea that the economy adapts to shifts in prices and is not manipulated through monetary policies. This represented a real departure from the idea of monetary sovereignty and a move away from the national currencies of the postwar period.[17]

To be eligible to adopt the euro, states had to agree to maintain exchange rates (within limits) with the euro for two years after adoption, keep inflation and interest rates close to those of the best performing member states, maintain their deficits below 3% of the country's gross domestic product (GDP), and keep their debt to less than 60% of GDP. These last two rules had to be maintained for the country to remain as a member of the EU. Perhaps most important, central banks producing currency should only lend as a last resort; the central bank should provide assistance to the commercial banks when needed, but at high interest rates.

This rule was broken in several instances in response to the financial crises in Greece, Ireland, Spain, and Portugal. Leaders have attempted to save failing states instead of eliminating them from the union by creating bailout funds, leading many economists to blame the crisis on a lack of central government tied to the euro instead of poor policy decisions. Again, the conceptual relationship between state and currency control remains intact for these economists. But we should note that part of the political motivation behind the creation of the euro was the idea of tightening the union between European states. In other words, its creation came about not through a nationalistic motivation, but a regional and geopolitical one. As Benjamin Cohen argues, "For all of the pact's insistence on formal legislation and golden rules, the same fundamental defect remains. Sovereign governments, ultimately, remain in charge of their own fiscal policy, which means once again that if push comes to shove, the pact's strictures may well prove unenforceable."[18]

While some imagined that the euro could prove a counterbalance to the US dollar as the world's reserve currency (the Organization of Petroleum Exporting Countries [OPEC] actually flirted with making the shift in the early days of the EU, a further sign of the connection between currency control and geopolitical power), this is now unlikely. But the US dollar is also in flux, based on the performance of the US economy and the nation's ever-rising national debt.

The real question is how long can this system last, and, perhaps more important, what will replace it and which forces could serve as an alternative? As Steil notes, "The dollar is ultimately just another money supported only by faith that others will willingly accept it in the future in return for the same sort of valuable things it bought in the past. This puts a great burden on the institutions of the U.S. government to validate that faith. And those institutions, unfortunately, are failing to shoulder that burden. Reckless U.S. fiscal policy is undermining the dollar's position even as the currency's role as a global money is expanding."

And so enter the cryptocurrency activists.

———

Early attempts to return to the age of fiduciary currencies and the gold standard were met with the full weight of the US fiat system. In 1998, Bernard von NotHaus sought to develop his own currency. He began making coins of gold, silver, platinum, and copper, and he called them Liberty Dollars.[19] Owners received electronic certificates representing the coins that they owned, which were stored in a warehouse in Idaho.

By 2009, when he was charged with "conspiracy against the United States" there were approximately 250,000 holders of Liberty Dollar certificates.[20] On March 18, 2011, Von NotHaus was convicted of "making, possessing and selling his own coins."[21] In particular, he was found in violation of 18 U.S.C. 486, which states, "Whoever, except as authorized by law, makes or utters or passes, or attempts to utter or pass, any coins of gold or silver or other metal, or alloys of metals, intended for use as current money, whether in the resemblance of coins of the United States or of foreign countries, or of original design, shall be fined under this title or imprisoned not more than five years, or both."

Another early attempt at digital currency was developed by a physician named Douglas Johnson. E-Gold was an electronic currency tied to the value of gold stored in locations around the world. It allowed people to make anonymous international transactions digitally. E-Gold attracted attention from the Department of Justice, and, in 2007, Johnson and two colleagues were charged with money laundering and operating an illegal business. James Finch, assistant director of the FBI's Cyber Division, said, "the advent of new electronic currency systems increases the risk that criminals, and possibly terrorists, will exploit these systems to launder money and transfer funds globally to avoid enforcement scrutiny and circumvent banking regulations and reporting."[22]

Drawing on a 1982 paper by computer scientist David Chaum, Bitcoin was the first significant effort to create an anonymous, cryptologically secure digital currency.[23] Previous digital currencies were backed by precious metals. Bitcoin is fully digital, and, despite attempts to find its creator—the anonymous computer programmer (or group of programmers) known by the pseudonym Satoshi Nakamoto—no state laws could be enforced against him (or them). The encrypted identities and peer-to-peer structure of the Bitcoin network mean that shutting down one part of the system will not disable the whole.

The authors of a 2013 report by the British think tank Demos on cryptocurrencies argue that "this decentralized system, where the minting of digital coins, the regulation of the currency and the prevention of fraud is based on mass participation makes Bitcoin independent from traditional financial mechanisms, or indeed any centralized control, in a way that other electronic cash systems never could be."[24]

Beyond being a technological leap beyond earlier experiments, Bitcoin was also a more defined political project. Early Bitcoin enthusiasts and developers saw it as an expression of digital libertarianism and a means of pushing back against state control of currency. Instead of entrusting governments, central bankers, and financial institutions to control currency, Satoshi Nakamoto built a system that allowed financial transactions to be guaranteed and tracked by a distributed network of computers solving complex math problems.

Nakamoto has described Bitcoin as a response to the inherent flaws in the financial system revealed during the 2008 financial crisis. Whereas early state-controlled currencies required and received the faith of their users (or citizens), Nakamoto argues that systems that depend on the trust of the state or a financial institution are inherently unstable and that the state could no longer be trusted to maintain the value of currency. In an early article on Bitcoin, he argued for a technological solution:

> What is needed is an electronic payment system based on cryptographic proof instead of trust, allowing any two willing parties to transact directly with each other without the need for a trusted third party. Transactions that are computationally impractical to reverse would protect sellers from fraud, and routine escrow mechanisms could easily be implemented to protect buyers.[25]

How does one create a currency without physical properties that is anonymous and not tied to the value of anything other than itself? At its core, Bitcoin is essentially just a list. It is a shared accounting ledger that consists of a fixed number of slots of code, each one of which is a "coin," and which can be purchased or traded. As Marc Andreessen describes it, "Anyone in the world can pay anyone else in the world any amount of value of Bitcoin by simply transferring ownership of the corresponding slot in the ledger. Put value in, transfer it, the recipient gets value out, no authorization required, and in many cases, no fees."[26]

Technically, the system is a bit more complex, particularly in how it replaces a central authority to guarantee the security of transactions with an ingenious distributed verification process. This process is described succinctly by economic journalist Tim Lee:

Whenever someone makes a Bitcoin transaction, the record of this transaction is submitted to the various nodes in the network. At fixed intervals, each node bundles up all the transactions it has seen into a data structure called a "block" and then races with the other nodes to solve a difficult mathematical problem that takes the block as an input. The first node to solve its problem (the problem is randomized in a way that gives each node a roughly equal chance) announces its success to the other nodes. Those nodes verify that all the transactions in the new block follow all the rules of the Bitcoin protocol, and that the solution to the mathematical problem is correct. . . . Once a winning solution is found, all nodes then treat the transactions encoded in the winning node's block as new entries in the global transaction register.[27]

The security of the transaction is therefore guaranteed and tracked by a distributed network of computers solving complex math problems. Whichever computer solves it gets a reward, and the act of problem solving ensures the security of the transaction. As an incentive to solve the math problems, each node in the network is allowed to add a reward to its efforts. If that node is the first to solve the problem, it is "minted" a fixed number of additional Bitcoins (currently set at 50). The reward for solving one of these problems is halved every four years, thereby limiting the number of new Bitcoins mined. Under this model, it will take approximately 100 years to reach a total of approximately 21 million Bitcoins.

Bitcoin replaces state oversight with the capabilities of a distributed network. Properly incentivized, this network ensures that coins are not copied or used twice. If you spend a Bitcoin, it cannot be returned. And while the value of a Bitcoin is not tied to a physical entity, it is also not purely a fiat currency, as the number of Bitcoins in circulation cannot be arbitrarily controlled. Unlike the US dollar, new Bitcoins cannot be either printed or taken out of circulation in order to adjust the currency's value, which is determined by a combination of the number of payments being made with it, the production of new coins in the problem-solving process, and speculation over its future value. So Bitcoin sits somewhat uncomfortably between a commodity and a fiat currency, an attribute that is the subject of significant critique, discussed later.

Bitcoin has some obvious practical applications, beginning with commercial services. For example, technologist

Chris Dixon has argued that Bitcoin could undermine the hefty transaction charges that banks place on the use of credit and debit cards and at point-of-sale terminals at retail outlets.[28] Fees of up to 5% can take a significant share of revenue, especially for low-margin businesses. Similarly, Marc Andreessen suggests that the low transaction costs of Bitcoin could facilitate online micropayments, perhaps finally enabling efficient online content markets. While these uses could drain the profits of the banking sector, if widely used they are unlikely to enable a revolutionary shift in power.

Bitcoin can also be used for remittances. Kenyans working abroad, for example, send roughly $1.2 billion back home each year through services such as Western Union and MoneyGram International Inc., which deduct substantial fees for each transaction, approximately $10 to $17 for a transfer of $200.[29] A new company called BitPesa will allow money transfers through Bitcoin and charge a fraction of those fees. As this market develops, money will be able to be transferred globally for almost no cost. An extension of this model is emerging whereby Bitcoin transfers can occur via M-PESA, a widely accepted currency transfer system over cell phones. M-PESA has over 18 million users in Kenya, and it is planning to integrate Bitcoin.

A range of new services can be built on the Bitcoin infrastructure. Bitcoin at its core allows one person on the Internet to transfer a unique digital property to someone else in a manner that is secure, anonymous, and reliable. Andreessen imagines that many forms of digital property would benefit from this network, including "digital signatures, digital contracts, digital keys (to physical locks, or to online lockers), digital ownership of physical assets such as cars and houses, digital stocks and bonds."[30]

The underlying Bitcoin ledger system can also be seen as a platform on which a host of services and tools can be built.[31] For example, Andreessen imagines the Internet of Things (think appliances connected to the Internet) using Bitcoin as a way of making purchases. Each appliance would have an identity on the distributed Bitcoin ledger and it could manage its energy purchases automatically.

But are these commercial utilities really the limit of the power of Bitcoin? It certainly is a far more limited view of its revolutionary potential than the ideological visions put forth by many early adopters. What is the potential for cryptocurrency, and is it a legitimate threat to state power?

————

Cryptocurrency is not without its critics. As the value of Bitcoin shot through the roof in late 2013, going from under $200 to a peak of $1,000, it burst into the popular discourse. Economist Tyler Cowen argues that the value of the anonymity of the model meant that there was reason to grant one-time seigniorage to the original issuers of the currency. At some point, though, this system will be replicable without the attached Bitcoin currency, meaning the value of the fiat currency will fall to near zero.[32]

In an article titled "Bitcoin, Magical Thinking and Political Ideology," programmer, writer, and angel investor Alex Payne sees Bitcoin as a sign of the disconnect between the boundless techno-optimism of Silicon Valley and the realities of the economic market.[33] He identifies this technologist exuberance with a libertarian ideology that is not concerned with addressing the structural systems that keep people in poverty, but rather focuses exclusively on freeing society from the reach of the state. This, he argues, is a fantasy that should be replaced by a focus on social services that "meaningfully and accountably improve our collective quality of life." Charlie Stross goes further and argues[34] that Bitcoin is just another form of tax evasion for the wealthy, further diminishing the ability of the state to provide social services.

Technology and economics journalist Timothy Lee identifies the potential for fraudulent collusion. If an individual user added 100 Bitcoins to the system as a problem-solving reward instead of the standard 50, that person would be rejected from the network. If a group of "rogue" nodes decided to collude and accept this reward, it could start a new community with higher rewards. A critical mass of users could collude to effectively change the rules of Bitcoin. Such collusion is both technically possible and, with increasing commercial interest in Bitcoin, becoming more likely.[35]

Bitcoin could be a bubble. Its position between a commodity and a currency and its fungibility make it subject to highly volatile speculation. As financial journalist Felix Salmon points out, "It's very hard to be a currency when you're also a commodity, governed by rules of scarcity and subject to speculative attack."[36] There is no central bank to regulate Bitcoin's value, nor a mechanism to inflate or deflate it. Whereas commodities can in theory have a stable value if the cost of production and storage remains flat, this is not guaranteed to be the case, and with shifting computing power, the cost of future Bitcoin mining remains uncertain. The current value of Bitcoin is therefore highly speculative, and likely unstable.

There is also a huge environmental cost to Bitcoin mining. This will only increase as the computations become more complex over time and the electricity needed to run the generators increases as the computational capacity soars. At a valuation of $1,000 per Bitcoin, the estimated carbon footprint of the electricity needed to run the mining ecosystem is 8.5 megatons per year, or 0.03% of global greenhouse emissions.[37]

There is a risk of Bitcoins causing hyperinflation. Suppose the value of a Bitcoin increases by 100 times. That would mean that a Bitcoin purchased for $100 would be worth $10,000. As the rest of the economy would not be inflating in the same manner, the Bitcoin with which you could once have bought goods worth $100—say, on Amazon.com—would now allow you to purchase goods worth $10,000. As the number of Bitcoins is fixed, there is no way of halting the inflation of a Bitcoin's value. You could, in theory, have hundreds of billions of dollars stored in Bitcoin. And this could in theory, result in a depression. Felix Salmon outlines the implication of this in the following manner: "In order to have economic growth, you need monetary growth as well—and that's something which is impossible to achieve in a Bitcoin-based system. Currencies such as the dollar, with a central bank which can print money at will, have succeeded for a reason. As economies grow, the money supply has to be able to grow with them."

Finally, the absence of the state in the oversight of Bitcoin use allows for dark markets to emerge. The more renowned to date was Silk Road, which was a free market for selling drugs and illegal services. But others have cropped up as well—including an exchange purported to sell assassinations.

Each of these critiques has been widely debated. And while they outline potential negative consequences, none of them restrict the Bitcoin network from existing. They do not, and cannot, shut it down. And this poses a real challenge for the states and institution that are threatened by its proliferation. It is precisely this reality that fuels many of the more radical cryptocurrency proponents.

———

Bitcoin was imagined and conceived as a radical opposition to state power. While there is increasing attention paid toward its practical commercial utility—and the significant Silicon Valley hype and funding that goes with it—there is a growing divide in the cryptocurrency community between those who want to normalize its use and those who remain steadfast in its revolutionary potential. It is the latter group that articulates a vision for cryptocurrency that is particularly relevant to state power and to the global financial system that it oversees.

The term "crypto-anarchy" was first coined by former engineer turned author Tim May and describes the state of lawlessness that could arise from more general use of encryption technologies. Crypto-anarchy, he argues, is "a throwback to the pre-state days of individual choice about which laws to follow."[38]

He argues that this manifestation of personal capability is one that is technologically enabled. "The technology for this revolution—and it surely will be both a social and economic revolution—has existed in theory for the past decade. The methods are based upon public-key encryption, zero-knowledge interactive proof systems, and various software protocols for interaction, authentication, and verification. . . . But only recently have computer networks and personal computers attained sufficient speed to make the ideas practically realizable."

Based on ideas of Ludvig von Mises, a group calling themselves the Mises Circle were early proponents of digital currencies, with a strong focus on individual liberty.[39] "Crypto-anarchy is not a branch of libertarian theory," they argue.[40] "It is a libertarian strategy. It is a framework for action. The cryptographic tools we have today are cheap, powerful, and profoundly individualistic. No one can hold a gun to an equation. Cryptographic software will function according to the rules of mathematics, regardless of government directives."

These are grandiose statements that many have marginalized. But they are grounded in attributes of cryptocurrency that are worth exploring. How does the design of Bitcoin challenge state power?

First, a central asset of Bitcoin is that it is anonymous. This allows for decentralized, seemingly formless financial transactions. Or, more specifically, it allows for information to be shared within a heavily encrypted network. In a very practical sense, this enables new forms of financial transactions. You don't need to know a seller's name, and he doesn't need to know yours. More important, this anonymity means there is no record of a transaction. This is problematic for the state control and regulation of both currency and markets. As Tim May states, "These developments will alter completely the nature of government regulation, the ability to tax and control economic interactions, the ability to keep information secret, and will even alter the nature of trust and reputation."[41]

Second, Bitcoin allows escape from the potential traps, or risks, of government-controlled currency. For example, Bitcoin is popular in Cyprus because, while its value is highly unstable, the government can't confiscate it or prevent you from sending it out of the country.[42] Similarly, if you live in a country at risk of hyperinflation, Bitcoin may be a legitimate way to opt out of your national currency. Salmon continues, "If you want to protect your wealth from the policies of your national government, or from the inflationary policies of a heterodox central bank, then Bitcoins can be a very good way of doing so in a largely undetectable manner."

The inverse is also true. Within the Bitcoin network itself, one is protected from artificial currency inflation (though not speculative valuation volatility). Whereas a government-based fiat currency can adjust valuation through injections of currency, making what you hold worth less, Bitcoin has no central authority that can change the model to allow for more Bitcoins to be produced. The rate of new Bitcoin production is based on a public algorithm.

This leads to a third attribute of Bitcoin's power—its decentralized collaborative nature. In fact, the technology of Bitcoin itself solves a core question of networked action. Namely, how do you create consensus in large-scale distributed anonymous systems without relying on any form of centralized authority? In short, every node in a Bitcoin network has an encryption key that can be verified (via the distributed problem-solving system) without the presence of a central authority.

Technologist and writer Paul Bohm argues that this ability for decentralized coordinated behavior is the central attribute on which Bitcoin's value will ultimately hinge: "If you think that we'll increasingly lose trust in the central authorities that manage the infrastructure we rely on, you might expect Bitcoins to rise a lot in value. If not, that is you believe that authorities will be able to tackle the challenges of the future better in centralized form, then from your perspective Bitcoins don't add value. We'll see."[43]

The degree of value one places in this decentralizing function is rooted in one's distrust of institutions. As Felix Salmon explains, this "built-in mistrust of institutions doesn't just set it apart from fiat currency, it also sets it apart from other virtual currencies, such as Facebook credits in the US, QQ coins in China, or Linden dollars in Second Life."[44] Most other digital currencies are embedded within the structure and particular interests of an institution. Bitcoin exists free of such constraints.

Bitcoin was initially born out of this mistrust. Satoshi Nakamoto claimed that Bitcoin was "completely decentralized, with no trusted authorities." He explained that this was due to a perceived reliance on trust for a conventional currency to function. The central banks must be trusted to keep the value of the currency and banks must be trusted to hold money, wisely invest it, and keep our privacy. History is replete with breaches of these trusts.[45]

Coming from the anonymous founder of a cryptocurrency, this argument could be seen as radical; but it is actually not that different from what Warren Buffett said to his shareholders in 2012:

> Investments that are denominated in a given currency include money-market funds, bonds, mortgages, bank deposits, and other instruments. Most of these currency-based investments are thought of as "safe." In truth they are among the most dangerous of assets. Over the past century these instruments have destroyed the purchasing power of investors in many countries, even as these holders continued to receive timely payments of interest and principal. This ugly result, moreover, will forever recur. Governments determine the ultimate value of money, and systemic forces will sometimes cause them to gravitate to policies that produce inflation. From time to time such policies spin out of control.[46]

If Bitcoin is designed to protect owners from the potential risk of government-controlled currency, it also is structured to exist out of the reach of the state. Because there is neither a central authority nor intermediaries between participants in a financial transaction (i.e., banks), then there is no point of interaction at which government can regulate. This means transactions can't be taxed or even monitored for criminal activity. It also means that the international legal system overseeing financial transactions is rendered futile. What's more, the distributed nature of the network means that finding and shutting down any one node will have no effect on the wider system. As with BitTorrent, there is no server you can turn off to make it go away.

If Bitcoin were to proliferate, this inability of the state to collect revenue and regulate commercial activity is a sure threat to the control it currently holds over the financial system.

———

The combination of encryption, "currency mining," and decentralized verification makes Bitcoin potentially powerful and difficult to control, but governments could do things to make the widespread adoption of Bitcoin problematic. They could enact laws, for example, that would all but remove it from US online commerce. The problem is that this technology is increasingly easy to deploy.

Investors like Marc Andreessen see Bitcoin as the future currency of the Internet, one that allows the simple exchange of value across borders. Bitcoin has the power to make remittances obsolete, undercut banks by decreasing

the cost of making online payments and transfers, and provide a native currency for the Internet of things (imagine
your washing machine paying its own electricity bill). They
want Bitcoin to be the next Paypal, with all of the initial
public offering (IPO) potential that will follow.

Under this model, a third-party service would hold your
Bitcoins (or e-wallets), connect with your bank account allowing for seamless conversion of Bitcoin to government-
issued currencies, and facilitate point of sale use of Bitcoins
via online tools and retail terminals. Companies are currently working with governments to establish this ecosystem within the current economic system. It would simply
be a cheaper and more efficient way of spending money—
hardly an anarchist's dream.

Faced with the choice of enabling the beneficial uses of
Bitcoin at the cost of proliferating its illicit uses, governments are unlikely to support its normalization into the
financial system. Without this support, Bitcoin as a mainstream currency is doomed.

Whether or not startup companies normalize their Bitcoin use with the government, nothing is stopping others
from existing outside of this model. For every one company
that wants to be the Bitcoin exchange for online retailers,
any number of others could seek to be the next Silk Road
or revolutionary currency.

Meanwhile, more radical technologies like Dark Wallet
are emerging; these offer a higher degree of anonymity
than more mainstream Bitcoin tools. Created by an anarchist group, Dark Wallet is an attempt to return Bitcoin to its radical and revolutionary roots. As stated on

a website promoting the technology, "Bitcoin is the next battleground in the fight against supranational political domination. Digital anonymity and freedom of financial speech are some of the last tools left in the dwindling garrisons of *Liberty*."[47]

Other groups seeking to undermine state power are also using cryptocurrencies. As National Public Radio (NPR) reported, the Oglala Lakota Nation in Idaho has just launched mazacoin as a means of increasing its independence from the US government.[48] The Oglala view currency control as an act of sovereignty.

How and whether Bitcoin itself succeeds, the disruptive power of alternative currencies is still significant, and we will certainly see new ones evolve using the technologies of early pioneers.

Put another way, the very attributes of cryptocurrencies that would allow Zimbabweans to protect their money from hyperinflation, Cypriots to prevent government seizure of their bank accounts, migrant workers to send money back to their families for free, or allow your fridge to pay its own bills also makes it impossible for governments to collect taxes, regulate international financial transactions, and monitor organized crime.

Bitcoin was imagined as a response to the tie between the state and money. It was invented as the financial lingua franca of the Internet—a currency born of, designed for, and using the attributes of the worldwide web. The very features that make it effective are also attributes that confound the state. Bitcoin is anonymous and decentralized. The state and its interaction with citizens is public and highly centralized. As such, Bitcoin allows for norms of behavior that sit outside the control of government. If the state loses control over the financial behavior of its citizens, it faces an existential crisis. On its surface then, Bitcoin must be viewed as a threat to state power.

CHAPTER FIVE

BEING THERE

Marie Colvin was the archetypal foreign correspondent. In temperament, bravado, ingenuity, and brash skill, she was, by all accounts, the embodiment of the wartime journalist. Throughout her career, she covered conflicts in East Timor, Libya, Sierra Leone, Zimbabwe, Kosovo, Chechnya, Iran, Iraq. She lost an eye to a grenade in Sri Lanka in 2001, and since then had worn a black patch.

Time and time again she would arrive somewhere at the peak of fighting and risk her life to relay stories to newspapers and television audiences largely in Western Europe and North America. Her capacity to get into tough places and her ability to tell stories of suffering, violence, tragedy, and horror, all with empathy, was revered and widely emulated. She was a window through which, we, as readers and viewers, experienced war.

In 2012, she was in Homs, a city on the front line of the Syrian war under siege by Bashar al-Assad. Colvin was the only British journalist bearing witness to the bombardment, which she described as the worst conflict she had ever experienced.

Colvin had snuck into Homs through a tunnel with the help of the opposition Free Syrian Army. A photojournalist working with her, Paul Conroy, had earlier told her that every bone in his body was telling him not to go back in. "Those are your concerns," she had responded. "I'm going in, no matter what. I'm the reporter, you're the photographer. If you want, you can stay here."[1]

On February 19, Colvin filed what would be her last dispatch for the *Sunday Times*. In it, she described the suffering in Homs in vivid emotional detail:

> They call it the widows' basement. Crammed amid makeshift beds and scattered belongings are frightened women and children trapped in the horror of Homs, the Syrian city shaken by two weeks of relentless bombardment.
>
> Among the 300 huddling in this wood factory cellar in the besieged district of Baba Amr is 20-year-old Noor, who lost her husband and her home to the shells and rockets. . . .
>
> For Noor, it was a double tragedy. Adnan, her 27-year-old brother, was killed at Maziad's side. "A baby born in the basement last week looked as shellshocked as her mother, Fatima, 19, who fled there when her family's single-storey house was obliterated. 'We survived by a miracle,' she whispers. Fatima is so traumatised that she cannot breastfeed, so the baby has been fed only sugar and water; there is no formula milk."
>
> Ali the dentist was cutting the clothes off 24-year-old Ahmed al-Irini on one of the clinic's two operating tables. Shrapnel had gashed huge bloody chunks out of Irini's thighs. Blood poured out as Ali used tweezers to draw a piece of metal from beneath his left eye. Irini's legs spasmed and he died on the table. His brother-in-law, who had

brought him in, began weeping. "We were playing cards when a missile hit our house," he said through his tears. Irini was taken out to the makeshift mortuary in a former back bedroom, naked but for a black plastic bag covering his genitals. . . .

On the lips of everyone was the question: "Why have we been abandoned by the world?"[2]

This striking piece of journalism accomplishes everything the form allows. It brings us into the conflict. It humanizes it. It reflects the scales, from personal to geopolitical, that the war represents. And it cost Colvin her life to tell it: an improvised explosive device (IED) killed her along with French photographer Rémi Ochlik.

Colvin's death shook me, not simply because she was uniquely accomplished or that her killing was the latest of a prominent journalist covering the Arab Spring, but also because of how the story of the Arab Spring, and particularly of Homs, unfolded for me. Whereas previous wars were broadcast on cable news and written about in print, I kept up with the Arab Spring news in real time on social media. Events were streamed live, both by those living through them and by a community of observers around the world. My Twitter stream was filled with real-time photos and videos of the conflicts, often in vivid and graphic detail.

While there has been much debate over the role of social media in the emergence of the Arab Spring movements, what is uncontested is that many of us followed them in a new way. For the Tunisian, Libyan, and Egyptian uprisings, this was largely via Twitter, either directly through citizen feeds or filtered through curators such as Andy Carvin of NPR, who pioneered a new form of virtual foreign correspondence. In Syria, and for the bombing of Homs that Colvin was covering, for the first time the world had plenty of video, live or nearly live, taken from mobile phones and posted to YouTube.

This allowed a graphic view of the conflict without the need for Western foreign correspondents to be brave enough (some would say reckless) to record it. The video form was decisively amateur. It was shot from rooftops and while running down the street. The quality was poor. But it was visceral and authentic in a way that is difficult for professionals to capture.

So unlike previous wars Colvin had covered, the bombardment of Homs, and indeed much of the Arab Spring, was being watched and lived via a range of new technologies. So maybe we did not need Marie Colvin and Rémi Ochlik to witness the bombing of Homs. They certainly provided a very different lens, Colvin in vivid prose, and Ochlik through beautiful, horrific images. And they provided a sense of the wider conflict, and of other conflicts, that could relay the war in a way that their Western viewers and readers, with similar backgrounds, could understand. But what if amateur representations of conflict were higher quality? Would that eliminate the need for foreign correspondents? How would that change how Western democracies understand and respond to war?

Or what if we could feel what it was like to be in Homs during the war? Danfung Dennis is an award-winning photojournalist and documentary filmmaker who has covered conflict for a decade. Having become frustrated with the limitations of photos and video, and in particular the distance between them and the events they depict, he left journalism to start a company called Condition One, which has developed a prototype virtual-reality camera and a headset that immerses the wearer in a 360 degree and three-dimensional (3D) video environment. It also has an app allowing users to move through a 3D environment using an iPad. Dennis says he wants to be able to better relay "what it's like to be there" and "to bridge the emotional gap between the story and ourselves." Recent experimentation in virtual reality journalism using 360 and 3D cameras and the Oculus Rift headset, including a project that I am involved in with at Columbia University, an interactive media company Secret Location, and the investigative documentary program *Frontline*, are pushing the boundaries of what it means to be immersed in a story.

Sam Gregory, the co-director of the human rights NGO Witness, believes that live video shot via wearable computers such as Google Glass and synchronous multi-sensory experiences can create an immersive experience that allows us to emotionally connect, to empathize with others in a way that fundamentally changes our understanding of one another. He calls this experience "co-presence for good," which he defines as "using the sense of being together with other people in a remote environment to drive concrete, productive actions, engagement and understanding across barriers of geography, exclusion and timezones."[3] Gregory is studying how real-time witnessing can be used to support activism, human rights advocacy, and the protection of rights defenders. And he is right to think that it might. A recent study by a team of Canadian psychologists found that social presence created by virtual reality can generate empathy akin to actually being there.[4]

We are certain to see the proliferation of virtual-reality technology and systems to carry cameras and microphones, including cheap, small, autonomous drones. It is very early for such technologies, and we certainly do not know whether they will lead to a better knowledge of events or change our actions in response to them. But they will surely change the role of reporters and the media institutions that support them. International reporting is more than just bearing witness. Journalists like Colvin interpret events and separate the signal from the noise of information. Both of these roles are more difficult to replace with technology. Now that technology can put us anywhere in the world, what do we need foreign correspondents for? Did Marie Colvin die for nothing?

―――――

In a 1787 speech to the British House of Commons while debating the merits of opening Parliament to the press, Edmund Burke introduced the concept of the Fourth Estate. Since then, whether it was Burke positioning the press as a force to counter the three pillars of parliamentary democracy, or the First Amendment to the US Constitution, signed two years after Burke's speech, guaranteeing the right to a free press, or Thomas Carlyle fifty years later pitting the press against the French church, nobility, and the townsmen, the Fourth Estate has come to represent a check against state power.

Through the 19th century, the capability, reach, and power of the press evolved along with technology. The laying of the first transatlantic cable in 1858 shortened communication time from Europe to America from 10 days to minutes, transforming what readers knew about the world. The proliferation of printing led to the creation of a multitude of small newspapers, a truly decentralized media ecosystem often serving communities of readers as small as a block or a streetcorner. In the 1890s, the United States had more than 14,000 weekly newspapers and nearly 2,000 dailies. And at the turn of the 20th century, as Western societies were industrializing, so too was the press—larger papers, then radio and television stations serving larger audiences with a wider range of interests.

The institutionalized press has always had a fraught relationship with the governments it was supposed to hold to account. In some cases, the state funded broadcasters like the British Broadcasting Corporation (BBC) in the United Kingdom or the Canadian Broadcasting Corporation (CBC) in Canada but mandated that they operate at arm's length from the providers of their funding. Independent corporate press also had a complicated role with state policy. In what has become media lore, upon hearing initial reports of calm from one of his journalists sent to Havana to cover the Spanish-American war in 1897, William Randolph Hearst replied, "Please remain. You furnish the pictures and I'll furnish the war." Often called the Yellow War due to the role of the press in instigating it, the Spanish-American War was nonetheless the first widely covered conflict, with Americans following new developments in each day's newspaper.

Until recently, we have been largely dependent on foreign correspondents to bear witness to war. Throughout the 20th century foreign correspondents have traded their independence for access and for protection from state combatants. Embedded reporting allows us into a conflict that is being fought on our behalf. But it does so at a cost, as reporters are being protected by the forces fighting one side of the war. In "The Dangers of Embedded Journalism, in War and Politics," national security reporter David Ignatius demonstrates how, following the first Gulf War, journalists approached the military for greater access to war zones so they could expand their reporting. The military agreed to this arrangement, since media offered a means of swaying public opinion in their favor and of controlling the narrative.

There was a cost to this access. US military explicitly sought to use embedded reporters to shift public opinion. As stated in a military guidance document on embedding, "Media coverage of any future operation will, to a large extent, shape public perception of the national security environment now and in the years ahead. This holds true for the US public, the public in allied countries whose opinion can affect the durability of our coalition, and publics in countries where we conduct operations, whose perceptions of us can affect the cost and duration of our involvement."[5]

Journalists and the media institutions that supported them were both to blame. Embedded journalists reported stories from their own eyes but often practiced self-censorship in order to craft a story that was more palatable for their audience or to protect the soldiers they traveled with. Additionally, interviews reveal that when embedded, journalists become more focused on telling their own story than a broader perspective of events. Truth becomes "their truth."

In turn, editors have their own subjective lenses. They want these reports to be exciting and entertaining to compete with other news outlets and magazines, yet not so real as to put off the audience. Editors also combine the embedded reports with those from "secondhand" reporters in the United States in order to present a balanced perspective.[6]

The end result is that too often embedding helps to develop a mutually beneficial relationship between the media and the military. Perhaps more worrying, this resulted in an increasing apathy of viewers/readers to foreign conflict, with Americans becoming desensitized to violence. The end result of greater access was a less engaged public.

As our eyewitnesses to global events, foreign correspondents have the authority of being there. Professor at the Annenburg School of Communications Barbie Zelizer sees eyewitnessing as a key traditional value of international journalism. In international reporting, significant influence extends from combining this witnessing with the subjective bias of the journalist and the audience's thirst for on-the-ground reporting. But this eyewitness role "extends journalistic authority in questionable ways," Zelizer claims, in that it "helps legitimate journalism in the popular imagination, but that legitimation is crafted through practices which journalism only partly implements."[7]

The images produced by international journalists have authority and power. Images and video tend to relay a kind of undeniable "truth," or the feeling of "being there." In this sense, foreign correspondents also represent values of "cosmopolitanism" as well as our own culture's ideas about the world. They allow the public to "see" events happening abroad but within the context and perspective of their home country.

The goal of a foreign correspondent is to report on the foreign while maintaining a familiar connection. As such, stereotypes and domestic concerns from the correspondent's home country often influence what is considered newsworthy. Usually, the correspondent will have only a few minutes on the air, so time for challenging assumptions is limited.

At the same time, economic changes in international news caused by the increase in online news consumption and decreasing revenue has led to substantive cuts in international news gathering. The expense of running foreign bureaus has meant many closures worldwide, especially since improvements in technology have made it possible for a single journalist to act as videographer, photographer, and live reporter. Both individual eyewitnesses as well as journalists without the support of media corporations can practice journalism from their phones. The result has been a shift in power from traditional media companies and the states they often became too close to, to a combination of citizen reporting, a new generation of digitally native journalists, and journalism organizations which look very different from the networks of old. The key question is, to what degree are they fulfilling the mandate of foreign reporting—to bear witness, add context, and find the signal in the noise?

——————

A jarring break in the slowly intersecting arcs of new and old media was the emergence of WikiLeaks, a website built to allow whistleblowers to anonymously and securely upload sensitive and revealing information. In many ways WikiLeaks embodies the attributes of disruptive power: It is anonymous, it facilitates the publication of information that is damaging to traditional institutions, and it seeks to operate outside global norms. It also wants to be considered a journalistic organization.

Initially WikiLeaks was treated as a cyber-activist organization and information source by other news outlets, but in 2010 it began trying to shift its image to that of a legitimate journalistic enterprise. The debate over whether WikiLeaks could be considered a journalistic organization began with its first major release, "Collateral Murder," which detailed a US helicopter attack on journalists on the ground in Iraq. WikiLeaks hosted the video on its own platform, accompanied by investigative reports from professional journalists it hired. Traditional news outlets did not approve, and WikiLeaks went back to releasing documents without any editorial annotation or collaboration with international news organizations. WikiLeaks was clearly innovative in its use of digital technology to make the secrets of governments visible.

On November 28, 2010, WikiLeaks released the largest batch of classified material in history, detailing communication among US consulates, embassies, and missions between 1966 and 2010. The data came to Wiki from a 23-year-old US Army private stationed in Iraq named Bradley Manning. (Manning has since changed gender and uses the name Chelsea.) Manning was not the first junior soldier to be troubled by the perceived abuses witnessed in war, but due to the nature of the US military's data sharing system and the service provided by WikiLeaks, she was able to leak massive amounts of sensitive data. Manning was ultimately charged with 22 crimes, including aiding and abetting the enemy, and sentenced to 35 years in prison.

WikiLeaks initially partnered with respected journalistic outlets for Cablegate, in large part to be legitimized. While Julian Assange, editor in chief of WikiLeaks, believed he too was a publisher, one who just happened to leak source documents, it is clear that the partner news organizations were never as convinced that WikiLeaks was a peer. To them, it was a difficult organization to categorize. WikiLeaks had originally partnered with the *New York Times, Der Spiegel,* and the *Guardian* to release files, but in 2010 the *Times* claimed that it saw WikiLeaks as more of a "source" than a partner.

But what is the difference in WikiLeaks publishing data and the *New York Times* publishing a leaked document? It is virtual, and core elements of its process have been technologically enabled. Recently, however, traditional media organizations such as the *New Yorker* and the *Guardian* have implemented similar anonymous document uploading tools.

A vocal proponent of treating WikiLeaks as a legitimate journalistic enterprise was Daniel Ellsberg, who leaked the Pentagon Papers to the *New York Times* during the Vietnam War. "Anybody who believes Julian Assange can be distinguished from the *New York Times*," he said, "is on a fool's errand."[8] Just as the US government attempted to suppress media coverage of the Pentagon Papers, now it was again attempting to delegitimize and suppress WikiLeaks. During Vietnam, the government failed when journalists convinced the public of the state's wrongdoing. In the case of WikiLeaks, the government seems to have partially succeeded in delegitimizing Julian Assange and his colleagues in the public's eyes.[9]

Regardless of labels, there can be little doubt that WikiLeaks and other technologies like it pose a challenge to traditional journalistic organizations, whose role has been as a buffer between events as they unfold, the powers that be, and citizens. Because Western societies have historically seen this role as important to our governance system, we have attributed certain powers and responsibilities to journalism. We traditionally gave them the power to disseminate information, via broadcast cables and print distribution channels; and in some cases, they had legal authority to protect their sources and hold illegal documents, with the expectation that editors would use information to benefit society. Now, if anyone can publish a leak, what is the role of journalistic institutions and the legal and regulatory protections we afford them?

Examples abound of digital media breaking down the traditional barriers between the press, the public, and the state. Pope Francis uses the handle @Pontifex to speak directly to his 4.7 million Twitter followers. Vice News and Buzzfeed report from front lines of warzones in a brash, first-person style that appeals to their millennial audiences. Edward Snowden leaked the NSA documents to Glenn Greenwald, a journalist and legal activist living in Brazil and blogging for the *Guardian*. Snowden says that he chose not to approach the *New York Times* because of its decision not to publish an earlier NSA domestic surveillance story in the lead-up to the 2004 election, after a request from the White House. But what if Snowden had given the documents to a blog on his brother's website? What if he had posted them to his own website?

After the billionaire co-founder of Ebay, Pierre Omidyar, considered buying the *Washington Post*, he instead invested the roughly $250 million that the purchase would have cost into a new media entity. Greenwald, one of Omidyar's first hires, sees this as a direct challenge to old journalism institutions: Activists and dissenters, Greenwald says, "are on the outside of institutional power, and what this is really about is being able to create a very well-funded, powerful, well-fortified institution that's designed not to just tolerate that kind of journalism, but to enable it and protect it, strengthen it and empower it."[10]

Yochai Benkler sees new digital institutions such as WikiLeaks as part of a Networked Fourth Estate. The new tools of digital technology have empowered citizens and individual journalists, and Benkler argues that WikiLeaks "forces us to ask how comfortable we are with the actual shape of democratization created by the Internet."[11] The Networked Fourth Estate is resilient in ways that traditional media companies are not. They exist across multiple jurisdictions and run mirrored sites (replicas of websites hosted on different servers), making them difficult to be shut down by any one government. They have networks of supporters willing to protect them through measures like DDoS attacks. They use mercenary tactics such as holding "insurance" files of unredacted data that they threaten to release if prosecuted, and they regularly mutate and replicate, making an attack on any one site futile. In short, they have disrupted both the traditional media outlets and the states that those outlets hold to account.

———

Had Marie Colvin been reporting from Syria 30 years ago, she would likely have been the only voice. We would have learned about the bombings via her prose. Twenty years ago, she might have been there with a cable TV network, broadcasting via satellite from a bombed out hotel. In 2012, she was there alone, with a small group of other professional journalists, and thousands of citizens uploading their accounts to Twitter and YouTube. We consumed the conflict in a new way because citizens could document it to the world alongside institutional journalists.

But what does this tell us about the existing power structures and norms of practice of the traditional media ecosystem detailed previously? How are digital media changing international journalism, and with it, our understanding of the world?

Large media organizations have held power over the global information environment through three levers of control: access to information, access to infrastructure, and the creation of journalistic norms. In each of these areas, digital technology is challenging the control held by the intersections of state and corporate interests that have long shaped the media narrative.

First, the media have historically had many ways of controlling, limiting, and shaping access to information. Some of this has to do with their ability to deploy resources—for example, the media and governments' mutually beneficial relationship when it comes to embedding journalists. The government allows the media access to information that the public would not otherwise receive. The media then function as a further gatekeeper, deciding what is news and what is not.

The concept of media "indexing" helps to further illuminate this relationship. In "Toward a Theory of Press-State Relations in the United States," political scientist and communications professor Lance Bennet argues that government has a privileged place in the structure of public debate. It provides access and feeds policy debates. However, the media, he argues, amplify this influence by deciding what is important based on the government's position. For example, in the media coverage of President Reagan's efforts to fund a war in El Salvador, Bennet found that the press framed the situation around the government's justifications, and significantly less reporting on the ongoing political situation was done after Congress stopped debating it. When official voices stopped commenting on it, so did the press. This indexing, based on access, is driven both by government's place at the center of democratic society and by journalistic norms of balance. As a result, governments and media together have traditionally played a significant role in deciding and shaping what debates citizens are exposed to and how they are framed.

Until recently, in order to tell a story of an event to the world, one needed both to be there and to have the platform through which to disseminate it. This meant that journalists working for media institutions were the people most likely to be present as events unfolded. There were always other people there, of course. They just didn't have the capability to broadcast what they were seeing. With the growth of the Internet and mobile computing, access to information is no longer monopolized. Nonprofessional journalists and citizens are finding their own stories by being in the right place at the right time. These eyewitness accounts do not necessarily help us understand and contextualize an event, but they do bring us there. These perspectives notably do not have the distance of professional journalism, nor do they attempt the objectivity to which the practice aspires.

Traditionally, mainstream news media have controlled the mass dissemination of information. Ownership of several platforms—newspapers, television networks, radio stations—allowed the voice of a single news outlet to spread quickly and efficiently. This arrangement also served to block out other voices. There has traditionally been a connection between access to distribution and editorial content production, and the media had a structural power over what information spread on the various networks. The reach of certain media conglomerates therefore gave them an authority over how debates are framed and what issues command the public's attention.

The former editor of *Foreign Affairs*, James Hoge, argues that in the international affairs space this leads to group-think and significant power for the media. "An overlooked aspect of media pervasiveness," he argues, "is its ability to quickly inform an audience swollen large in times of crisis. At such moments the massive flow of information will contain the sound and the unsound, the responsible and the irresponsible."

Anyone can now disseminate information on a new media infrastructure. Blogs, social networks, and the wider Internet all allow people to self-publish and have the capacity to reach most people around the globe. Mainstream news no longer has a monopoly on disseminating mass information. However, mainstream news networks have also adopted these formerly alternative online devices, resulting in an integration of old and new forms.

Several years ago, a 21-year-old student at Istanbul's Bahçeşehir University named Engin Onder co-founded 140 Journos, an organization whose volunteers use their own mobile devices to provide uncensored news to the public via social media platforms like Twitter and SoundCloud. Named for the 140-character limit on Twitter, 140 Journos has never consisted of more than 20 people, and yet it has had a marked impact on the closed and controlled Turkish media that regularly imprisons citizens for certain types of speech. "We are all journalists now," Onder explained to the *Columbia Journalism Review*. "What we have is our own devices. . . . [I]t actually removes the barriers between the person who sees the news and [the one] who creates the news."[12]

Despite a plethora of new platforms, tools, and sharing methods, Director of the MIT Civic Media Lab Ethan Zuckerman argues that we remain drawn to local sources of information in our day-to-day life. Sites like Kigali Wire and MexicoReporter.com represent a new way of reporting local news to an international audience using a variety of digital tools. The new platforms have now replaced the demand for professional journalists, leading to greater cuts to the industry and to many outlets depending on just news wires like the Associated Press and Reuters.[13]

In the past, elites in the media network have had the ability to establish norms to be followed by the rest of the network. Social practices of journalism evolved over time and across news outlets, creating strong norms of behavior. In this way the news media could be viewed as a collective with a standard set of roles and practices. This homogeneity of journalistic behavior and coverage has had real consequence for the limited frames through which we traditionally saw the world and stands in marked contrast to the diversity of voices and stories that the new digital media ecosystem allows.[14] Due to the decentralization of access to information and the ability for anyone to broadcast, norms are breaking down and new ones are forming. Social networks have been critical in the development of a rapidly evolving new set of journalistic practices and values that are reinventing how the news is relayed.[15]

Take the norm of purported journalistic objectivity, which lies in stark contrast to the online world. If I am writing a blog or live-tweeting, my subjectivity is explicit. Even if I am filming an event on my phone, any number of my personal and situational biases are embedded in my documentation. My choice of what to film, of how to position and edit the video, and whether to broadcast it at all are just some of the subjective elements that enter into citizen journalism.

This shift in the norm of objectivity, which is itself a 20th-century construct, has also been found among professional journalists who blog. Professor of entrepreneurial journalism Jane Singer has studied how the mainstream press are adopting previously alternative online media.[16] She found that the behavior of journalists changes online. Journalists often shift to the first person and reflect on stories in a manner not generally adopted in print or by broadcast outlets. On blogs, the traditional gatekeeping role of the journalist shifts to one of information verification and quality control. The norms of blogging, therefore, are driving behavioral change.

Another strong new norm emerging is instantaneity. In a recent study of social media storytelling during the Egyptian uprisings, Zizi Papacharissi and Oliveira de Fatima analyzed and mapped information flows over Twitter during the Egyptian uprisings as a way of looking at the changing dynamic of news. They found that social streams reflect sets of "news values" different from those of traditional media. On Twitter, values centered on instantaneity, solidarity, and information from trusted elites. The differences in these "organically" emergent values from those of traditional media indicate how media norms can change over a short period of time, diminishing the power of mainstream media as an enforcer of media norms.[17]

The structural power traditionally held by the media to shape and disseminate news about the world and the limitations of the individual foreign correspondent as a conduit to global events have now met the radically disseminated world of digital media. The resulting power shift from media companies and their institutional norms to individuals in the production and destination of news is a major change in the international system. This new media ecosystem is far more decentralized, gets news of events to us quicker than before, and is less vulnerable to the current decline in traditional media revenue models or shifts in domestic political pressures. This is surely a good thing.

But do these new norms represent a shift in power? Media theorist Manuel Castells believes so. Social movements are organized not only in a digital space but also in a flow of information existing through networks, face-to-face interactions, and traditional media. They are not completely divorced from real-world foundations but have lost their fragmented nature and now exist in a global network. This is a network that is harder to control than media infrastructure.

To Castells, power is defined as the ability of one actor to control another actor, and counterpower as the ability of an actor to resist institutional power. A move toward citizen journalism and away from institutionally produced media, is, for him, a form of "socialized communication." In this new ecosystem, traditional "vertical" forms of communication are replaced by horizontal networks (or the Internet), and with this shift comes a challenge to the ability of any one organization to control information. The disruption of the ability to control information, whether by corporate, media, or political elites, is for Castells a form of counterpower.[18]

This counterpower is by no means absolute. As we have seen with the scale of state surveillance and the degree of cooperation by the telecommunication and technology companies that operate the infrastructure of our global communications, there is a fight for this ability to control and monitor information. As we have explored, there is a booming private-sector industry in providing technologies for countries, both autocracies and democracies, to control the Internet. But this is an exertion of power in response to the communication capabilities afforded through it.[19]

———

So where does this leave the media landscape as it relates to international journalism? Are we heading toward a world where citizen-led media cut out the traditional broadcasters and broadsheets? In international journalism, is it better for us to learn about the world through those who are living through events as they unfold? Or would we rather continue to have the world told to us through the lens of a trusted observer?

We are seeing a new dynamic ecosystem of information sharing. Some of this information comes from professionals, some directly from sources, and others from people documenting the lives they are living. Journalist and scholar

Paulo Nuno Vicente recently conducted a study of international reporters based in Nairobi to investigate their experiences with being part of online media, how they translate their perspective into their reporting, and how they view the rise of citizen journalism. Most of the reporters were aware that they were no longer leading journalism in the digital age. Many still attempted to draw borders between amateur and professional journalism, underlining the quality and accuracy of their work. However, many believe the two groups can be partners in the telling of international stories, each bringing a different perspective to the table. In this view, more traditional journalists such as Colvin can see themselves adding value and context to the flow of social media information.[20]

Did Marie Colvin die for nothing? No, we still need observers and explainers immersing themselves in places and contexts which we citizens cannot ourselves know. But our ability to learn about events by other means is rapidly increasing. Our ability to watch from afar will only increase when we are able to immerse ourselves in virtual reality and real-time social video, or go anywhere a camera on a micro-drone will take us. Bearing witness is no longer sufficient to justify the risks correspondents take. And traditional journalistic roles—providing context and separating signal from noise—are being replaced by new digital tools and crowd-sourced platforms.

And this has implications for both the state and traditional media companies, both of which have gained power and influence through their capacity to control information. Perhaps more crucially the traditional media and the legal and regulatory system that support it (however imperfect) have for over a century provided a check on power. Digital technology has, in effect, democratized the Fourth Estate and as such, the public now bears more responsibility than ever for holding power to account. It is yet to be seen whether this will be a truly democratizing shift or whether the state will be able to fight back though surveillance, secrecy, and force.

CHAPTER SIX

SAVING THE SAVIORS

On December 27, 2007, Kenya held a presidential election. The declared winner was President Mwai Kibaki, but opposition supporters and international monitors disputed the results, and ethnic violence broke out. Ory Okolloh, a Kenyan lawyer and blogger who lives in South Africa but had returned to her native land to vote, faced threats to her life. Back in South Africa, she had an idea for a platform called Ushahidi, the Swahili word for "testimony," that would allow Kenyan citizens to anonymously report incidents of violence. An ad hoc group of technologists with ties to Kenya saw Okolloh's post and built Ushahidi in a matter of days.

Ushahidi allows data to be uploaded to a live map via text message, email, or online entry. An open-source platform, Ushahidi was adapted for crowdsourced mapping projects beyond the Kenyan electoral crisis. A Kenyan wildlife group used it to track animal sightings, Al Jazeera used it during the 2009 Gaza War, and an initiative called HarassMapp uses the Ushahidi platform to map reports of sexual assault in Egypt. But Ushahidi came to global prominence after the January 12, 2010, earthquake in Haiti.

Already one of the poorest countries in the world, Haiti had not been hit by a large earthquake since 1842, and most of the population of the capital city, Port-au-Prince, lived in slum conditions in poorly constructed buildings. More than 100,000 houses were destroyed as were 60% of government buildings; destruction of this magnitude gutted the state's already limited capacity to respond to a natural disaster. An estimated 220,000 people were killed, including 25% of all civil servants, and 300,000 more were injured. More than 1.5 million people were housed in temporary camps that were vulnerable to aftershocks, flooding, disease, and crime. International humanitarian organizations mobilized to move into Haiti and provide assistance, but information on who needed help, and where, was hard to find. The Haitian government had not kept detailed population records, and basic street maps were non-existent.

Patrick Meier, at the time a PhD student at the Fletcher School of Law and Diplomacy, had friends in Haiti, and he followed news about the earthquake closely.[1] Starting with tweets by a dozen people in Port-au-Prince, Meier used Ushahidi to create a map of Haiti from Cambridge, Massachusetts. Some tweets contain geolocation data, which can be collected and mapped in real time. Meier began following more Haitian Twitter handles, and he incorporated text messages so that anyone with a cell phone could upload information to the map. First, texts came from the Haitian Diaspora and then, through a partnership with the Haitian telecom Digicel, directly from Haiti via a toll-free SMS (Short Message Service) shortcode. Word spread and, within days, thousands of text messages reporting needs and locations came in. (Most texts were in Haitian Creole, and Meier set up a second platform to facilitate the crowd-sourced translation of incoming text messages.) Meier enlisted more than 100 fellow students in the effort. Calling themselves "digital humanitarians," they tracked social networks and mainstream media for any relevant information that could be added to the rapidly evolving map.

Since Google Maps hadn't yet covered Port-au-Prince, they turned to OpenStreetMap, another open-source project, whose volunteers created a draft map by downloading satellite images of Haiti and tracing streets and buildings. Data uploaded by volunteers using global positioning system (GPS) devices on the ground filled in the Open-StreetMap. Within several weeks, people around the world edited the map nearly 10,000 times, and the crisis response community had a useful map of the affected region.[2] The US Department of State, US Marines, US Coast Guard, the International Red Cross, and a wide array of smaller non-profit humanitarian organizations as well as private citizens used the map to target relief. The Federal Emergency Management Authority endorsed the map as the most accurate and up-to-date source of information on Haiti available to the humanitarian community.

In a Technology, Entertainment, Design (TED) talk about digital humanitarians, Paul Conneally, communications manager for the International Federation of the Red Cross and Red Crescent Societies, presents the earthquake in Haiti as a catalyst for change in the humanitarian community. "Right across the developing world," he proclaimed, "citizens and communities are using technology to enable them to bring about change, positive change, in their own communities. The grassroots have been strengthened through the social power of sharing and they are challenging the old models, the old analog models of control and command."[3]

In a blog post, Meier described how platforms like Ushahidi can be useful not just in emergencies but as a tool for civil society as a check on governments, what he called "sousveillance."[4] Collecting data and publishing maps were once the sole privilege of the state, but as Meier argues, the Ushahidi platform provides a participatory digital canvas for the public decoding, recoding of information and synchronization of said information. In other words, the platform serves to democratize dataveillance by crowdsourcing what was once the exclusive realm of the "security-informational complex." With Ushahidi, "the barriers to entry are now very low," Ushahidi staffer and developer David Kobia adds. "The aim is really to push the power down to the masses." Anyone with a computer and an Internet connection can create a Ushahidi map.

They do need to be connected though. And increasingly in developing countries, this connectivity is provided by large multinational technology companies such as Google and Facebook, who see global Internet access as a tool for economic development. They could well be right, but the access they are providing comes at a cost, whether it be having to use Facebook as a portal to the Internet, or new systems of micropayment and micro lending. As Facebook CEO Mark Zukerberg said about Internet.org, a group he started to bring Internet access to the developing world, the goal is to show "people why it's rational and good for them to spend the limited money they have on the Internet."[5]

Ushahidi's work had a significant impact on the Haitian crisis and beyond. It has helped individuals and grassroots volunteer networks get involved in formal international development contexts. It is far more organized than groups such as Anonymous and Telecomix; in a paper on the use of sophisticated volunteer networks, Meier describes teams for media monitoring, geolocation, verification, and analysis. Like an early disruptive innovator, Ushahidi has found a capability ignored by the dominant actor (in this case, large international organizations and government development agencies) and are now growing the capacity to challenge their control of the space.[6]

Two years after the initial uses of the Ushahidi platform in the post-Kenyan election violence, one of the cofounders of the project, Erik Hersman, a technologist and a blogger living in Florida but raised in Kenya and Sudan, moved back to Nairobi to start an innovation hub. He believed that the technology and start-up community in Kenya would benefit from a shared innovation space. The space, called iHub, would serve as both Ushahidi's home and a place for a wide range of technology companies and programs meant to develop Kenya's technology sector and connect developers and researchers with potential funding. It is primarily an incubator and offers free access to 100 entrepreneurs who have competed for spots.

For example, one project to come through the iHub program is called M-Farm. Launched and built by three young women after winning a 48-hour start-up competition, M-Farm is a text message-based information tool for farmers. It allows them to get access to up-to-date retail pricing for their products and helps them to find buyers and to make purchases, in theory cutting out middle men and giving farmers agency over pricing.[7] The realities of deploying a mobile software solution to what is a widespread structural challenge in one of the world's 30 poorest countries, where more than half the population lives below the poverty line of US$1 per day, are daunting.

Whereas the Ushahidi platform has been used mostly for crisis scenarios, iHub's desired impact can be far more broadly defined. Its creators are aiming to create high value-added jobs for young Kenyans in the technology sector; they are stimulating venture capital investment in a new start-up ecosystem, and they are attracting significant investment from corporate sponsors. But they are not just seeking to create economic growth; iHub's proponents also make claims as to the values and impact of the technologies themselves. M-Farm is promoted as a technological solution to a development challenge as well as an employment initiative for its founders. What's more, both Ushahidi and iHub are seeking to innovate in two spaces, humanitarianism and development, long controlled by the state and large international organizations.

———

The history of aid is rife with conflict among states, the institutions and people delivering assistance, and the people in need. The origins of humanitarian aid are often traced to Florence Nightingale's treatment of the wounded in the Crimean War in the middle of the 19th century. Working with small groups of volunteer nurses whom she trained, Nightingale pleaded with the British government for a state solution—the creation of prefabricated hospitals that could be sent to the front lines. This notion of helping others while conquering them is of course closely tied to the economic and political history of European colonialism.

At around the same time, a non-government humanitarian movement was growing. The International Committee of the Red Cross was founded in Switzerland in 1863, and the American Red Cross 20 years later. Both experienced rapid growth and had massive humanitarian impact during World War I. In America alone, by 1918 the organization had 3,864 local chapters and 20 million members. It was a tangible way in which citizens could help in the war being fought a world away.

Following the Second World War, aid industrialized and notably became tied up in the development of global financial institutions. The creation of the United Nations, the International Bank for Reconstruction and Development (IBRD or World Bank), and the International Monetary Fund (IMF) as well as state development agencies came about with the mixed mandate of promoting Western economic growth and capitalist expansion while also raising incomes and creating economic stability, and assisting with the industrialization of the developing world. Aid and development were caught in the mixed motives of the state—and of what many would call a new form of economic colonialism.

At the same time, an entire industry of independent humanitarianism emerged. International organizations like Oxfam, Care, Save the Children, and World Vision grew into large bureaucratic organizations delivering aid mainly from citizens of the West to those in need in the developing world.

As human rights scholars Margaret Satterthwaite and Scott Moses argue, "The expansion of the [international non-governmental organization] INGO sector can be usefully understood as—among other things—a form of outsourcing by Western and Northern donor states. Where in the past, Western states governed directly via colonialism and indirectly via Cold War-era neocolonialism, now Western states outsource certain governance activities in the Global South to development and humanitarian INGOs."[8] Essentially, INGOs can act as de facto governments and agents of the Western countries that fund them. As they have large budgets and better resources, in countries like Haiti they can achieve more legitimacy than the actual government.

During the 1980s and 1990s, many developing countries had little choice but to follow economic policies imposed by donor countries. This frequently included the widespread deployment of Western technologies and IT infrastructure, often designed for purposes far different from the actual development priorities of the receiving country, such as improvements in agriculture, medicine, water and sanitation, energy, and ways to fight the spread of disease.[9] It would of course be far more advantageous to incorporate local priorities at the start of the technology development processes, but the nature of the aid system, whether it involves food aid, farming equipment, or information technology, privileges the economic benefits of the donor over those of the recipients.

Even before the widespread adoption of the worldwide web and mobile telecommunication, advances in information technology changed the practice of international humanitarian efforts, particularly around disaster management and planning.[10] Administrative applications for desktop computers gave field operations more independence in refugee food programming, project management, and commodity tracking.[11] Humanitarians were early adopters of email and computerized bulletin boards. Humanitarian institutions shed middle management layers, and the pace of international operations sped up with Telexes and fax machines. Systems such as the Famine Early Warning, created in 1985 by the US Agency for International Development (USAID), provided the ability to collect and analyze large datasets with the goal of predicting the onset of humanitarian emergencies.

Mapping was also once solely the purview of the state, and thus closely aligned with state interests. The evolution of cartography can be closely linked to technological development. Political scientist Jordan Branch has argued that the use of early technologies for mapping, such as the compass, quadrant, printing press, telescope, and sextant, was a fundamental driver of the development of modern territorial state system. These new tools, he argues, "altered how political actors understood political space, authority, and organization, reducing the wide variety of medieval political forms down to the unique territorial form of the sovereign state."[12]

The 20th century saw the advent of aerial photography, satellite technology, remote sensing, and geographic information systems (GIS), all of which were in large part developed and funded by the state, often for military purposes. The history of GIS is particularly closely tied to the state, first for land use planning, and then in the late 1960s and after widely used for military planning and targeting. By the mid 1990s, desktop GIS programs were available, and the use of digital mapping across the private sector proliferated. It was mapping moving to the cloud, however, that caused a revolution in how we use maps.

Google Earth was launched in June 2005 after Google acquired a program funded by the Central Intelligence Agency (CIA) called EarthViewer 3D. The desktop and mobile program uses satellite imagery, aerial photography, and GIS-based 3D imagery to create a simulation of the world that can be explored with remarkable detail and precision. The potential humanitarian uses of Google Earth quickly became clear. Based in part on Google's experience mapping the damage from Hurricane Katrina, in 2007 the company launched Google Earth Outreach, and what they call Google Earth Awareness Layers, which used the slogan, "You want to change the world. We want to help."

One pilot project, a partnership with the United States Holocaust Memorial Museum's Genocide Prevention Mapping Initiative, documented war crimes in Darfur, a region of western Sudan where the government was engaged in an ethnic-cleansing campaign. "Crisis in Darfur" brought

together high-resolution satellite imagery, geo-tagged photographs, and written testimony collected by Amnesty International. The resulting interactive map captured images
of villages burned and of vast refugee camps, and it allowed visitors to learn about the crisis in a new and visceral way. As Catherine Summerhayes, a lecturer in Film
and New Media Studies at Australian National University,
wrote:

> When I see the flames of "Crisis in Darfur" growing larger
> on my computer screen as I roll my mouse towards a closer
> focus, I feel a sense of dread and fascination. Why fascina-
> tion? Perhaps it is not only towards a spectacle of destruc-
> tion in which happily I am not directly involved (as in the
> experience of car accident gazing). Perhaps such a fascina-
> tion and dread is also a result from recognition through
> "sympathetic identification."[13]

All Eyes on Darfur, sponsored by Amnesty International, monitored attacks in real time, using satellite data
from three private companies—Digital Globe, Geoeye,
and Imagesat—to monitor 13 vulnerable villages. There
was also an attempt to spatially analyze this real-time data
to predict other villages that might be at risk of attack.[14]

Then actor George Clooney along with John Prendergrast of the Enough Project conceived of and funded the
Satellite Sentinel Project. The Satellite Sentinel Project
seeks to serve as an early warning system for mass atrocities on the border between Sudan and what is now South
Sudan, using regularly updated satellite imagery from

DigitalGlobe. The point, Clooney says, was to focus on Sudanese troops "the level of celebrity attention that I usually get. If you know your actions are going to be covered, you tend to behave much differently than when you operate in a vacuum."[15] Real-time monitoring and the ability to amplify findings via the combined media power of Clooney and the Enough Project is a powerful combination.

In one case, Satellite Sentinel Project analysts, based in Cambridge, Massachusetts, saw what appeared to be 3,000 Sudanese troops readying an attack on a village named Kurmuk on the border of South Sudan; they published the news to give the villagers a chance to flee, potentially shifting the outcome of a crisis on another continent. As director of the Sentinel Project Nathanial Raymond reflected, "What if we get the direction the force is going wrong? You could have walked the civilian population right into them." We don't know how many people were warned of the attack, but the village was ultimately taken over by the army and used as an airbase.[16]

Projects like All Eyes on Darfur and Satellite Sentinel say that they make a difference in humanitarian interventions. They seek to change the behavior of would-be war criminals by raising the visibility and potential costs of their actions, building on an idea first proposed at the US-Soviet Summit meeting in 1960 by President Dwight Eisenhower for a UN-operated aerial surveillance system to detect preparations for bombing attacks. The Soviets had recently shot down a CIA spy plane and Eisenhower was willing now to allow a system of international surveillance that would negate the need for national espionage.

While the Russians dismissed this proposal, 40 years later the UN did set up its own satellite surveillance unit, called the UN's Operational Satellite Program, which is used to analyze patterns of attack in conflict.[17]

These satellite projects all seek to raise awareness in the West about humanitarian crises. As John Prendergrast puts it, "No one can any longer say they don't know. This tool will bring a spotlight to a very dark corner of the earth, a torch that will indirectly help protect the victims. It is David versus Goliath, and Google Earth just gave David a stone for his slingshot."[18] And the hope is that more and better information about humanitarian crises will lead to better policy decisions.

However, despite exuberant proclamations about how Google Earth Awareness Layers provides "collaborative and dynamic ways for communities to come together, share critical information, and help citizens see the world in a new light," there is little evidence for any of these claims.[19]

Amnesty argues that the government of Chad cited the All Eyes on Darfur project as a reason it accepted UN peacekeepers. Yet while the villages they were monitoring were not attacked, neighboring ones were, and war continues.[20] Two years after the earthquake in Haiti, more than half a million people remained homeless, most living in tents in camps for internally displaced persons. Unsanitary living conditions led to a cholera epidemic, affecting 5% of the population. The Haitian government is in disarray, and foreign governments, international humanitarian organizations, and corporations have largely pulled out of the country.

How are we to make sense of this emerging space? It seems filled with promise, idealism, and the rhetoric of liberation. Is it possible for digital technology-enabled initiatives to change the space of humanitarianism and shift power from the state and established NGOs to networks of individuals? Can digital humanitarian programs be more effective and empowering to the intended recipients of aid? Or do these technologies replicate the power structures of the traditional aid paradigm, and continue to propagate representations of victimhood?

———

The term "information and communications for technologies for development" (ICT4D) emerged from development research in the 1960s and 1970s suggesting that societal technological development can have an instrumental effect on development outcomes. Initially, ICT4D initiatives involved the funding and construction of electrical grids and telecommunications systems through state to state aid. With the rise of the Internet, these programs evolved to include Internet access programs and any number of "e" initiatives; e-health, e-government, e-agriculture, e-learning, e-security. Now the attention has shifted to mobile technology and the use of satellites, artificial intelligence, and drones, all for humanitarian and development ends. There has been a new push to invest in and build the next generation of ICT infrastructure, whether for mobile communications or for wireless Internet, such as Facebook's drone Internet program and Google's balloon Internet initiative. In 2010, Africa as a continent spent over $60 billion on ICT infrastructure, the equivalent of about $60 per person.[21] The same year, the World Bank spent over $800 million on ICT development, and the private sector invested over $10 billion in mobile infrastructure alone. Individuals are also spending a huge amount to be connected. Apart from the richest quintile, Africans who own mobile phones spend 11% to 27% of their monthly income on them.[22]

Throughout this evolution, the critiques have remained consistent—information technology initiatives, many argue, simply mask the core structural causes of underdevelopment, poor health outcomes, struggling agricultural sectors, and poverty. Critics charge that they are a Western-driven fix that is imposed outside of local development contexts and are based on a neo-liberal notion that greater access to technology and commerce will lead to economic growth and ultimately development.

In a 1999 paper reviewing the empirical work on the connection between adoption of ICTs and development indicators, economist Arjun Bedi said the obvious: "Proponents attribute a wide and almost impossible array of positive effects to ICTs."[23] Even a cursory scan of the popular press, think tank papers, and reports from international development organizations reveals a laundry list of utopian outcomes: stimulating economic growth, saving citizens in emergencies, preventing crimes against humanity, revolutionizing agriculture, bringing medical care to the rural poor, revealing government corruption, saving and spreading democracy.

Despite the overwrought rhetoric, good can come from the adoption of new technologies. One of the challenges in exploring their impact, however, is that many conversations and objectives merge, and talk of digital humanitarianism gets entwined with economic development efforts by governments, telecommunications companies, and venture capital firms. Ushahidi, for example, has become part of iHub, which has a mandate for both creating local jobs in the technology sector and solving national development problems with digital technology.

There is a significant literature on the impact of information technology on the practice and outcomes of human development, much of which is outside the bounds of this analysis. However, a brief look is valuable to see how its adoption, in development institutions and in the communities they serve, is leading to institutional change, empowering individuals in developing areas, and fueling economic growth.

Arjun Bedi notes that lower transaction costs create opportunities for disruptive innovators, forcing inefficient organizations to adapt, and widespread knowledge about new technologies allows them to compete. Indeed, institutions from the World Bank (its Open Data Initiative provides free access to almost all of their data and invites application developers to use this data to create development-focused applications) to the United Nations (its Digital Pulse network of innovation labs works to use real-time data to address potential global crises such as famines and epidemics) to USAID (its Development Innovation Ventures funds development start-ups focused on humanitarian and development goals) are trying to embrace the new land-scape. Whether these established institutions can innovate in the wider humanitarian effort remains to be seen.

There is an extensive literature on how digital technol-ogy empowers individuals, promotes good governance, and enables political resistance to autocratic regimes.[24] Po-litical scientist Guy Grossman argues that ICT adoption is leading to new forms of direct political participation that is restraining elite opinion and behavior. In a paper on the effects of digital technology adoption in Africa, anthro-pologist Gado Alzouma sees "an opportunity for shifting and sharing power until now concentrated in the hands of the urban political authoritarian elite . . . to empower rural and poor people through the use of information technologies."[25]

Still, Manuel Castells argues that communication tech-nologies are a double-edged sword. They can allow societ-ies to leapfrog stages of development, as occurred in Hong Kong, Taiwan, Singapore, Malaysia, and South Korea.[26] But if a country does not have the education system or other social and political conditions needed to capitalize on new technologies, then it can be locked out of the benefits en masse. "Technology per se does not solve social problems," Castells concludes,[27] "But the availability and use of infor-mation and communication technologies are a pre-requisite for economic and social development in our world. They are the functional equivalent of electricity in the industrial era."

"The humanitarian model has barely changed since the early twentieth century," Paul Conneally says.[28] "Its ori-gins are firmly rooted in the analogue age, and there is a major shift coming." The catalyst for this shift, he argues, was the 2010 Haiti earthquake.

What exactly is new about digital humanitarianism? The innovations around maps are the result of several core advances in online programming, such as the availability of cartographic APIs (application programming interfaces) and GPS-enabled mobile phones, and communities are emerging around this new technology that are able to do things in the humanitarian space that were simply not possible before.

These communities can do things that traditional humanitarian organizations cannot. In Haiti, where traditional organizations needed field offices or advance teams to get information, crisis maps are almost immediately deployable. While traditional organizations could use Ushahidi maps, a culture of risk avoidance makes using and publishing crowdsourced data very difficult.

What's more, large humanitarian organizations saw information technology the way states and traditional media organizations did: as a means to enhance their control over the dissemination of information, not as a means for two-way communications. As Gloria Huang from the American Red Cross told journalist Katie Collins, "While they were prepared to broadcast information about the disaster and what the agency was doing through blogs and social media, what they were not prepared for was the influx of posts and messages from people who were suffering, or who knew people who were suffering."[29]

Once a humanitarian operation is opened up to public participation, it empowers a wide range of new actors and privileges new sources and forms of data. Individuals affected by the crisis can share information with one another, and they can communicate directly with the outside world.[30]

It is difficult to overemphasize how the ability of individuals to report directly on their own condition in real time changes the information environment for humanitarian organizations. In some potentially very powerful ways, this can serve to transfer ownership and power over aspects of the humanitarian space to those whose lives are being affected. In the case of the text message campaign in Haiti, this meant transferring the event reporting and translation services to local Haitians soon after the system was launched. These intertwined technologies lead to new mixes of authoritative and non-authoritative data, which rapidly can become a complex mix of data streams, types, and sources. This then is an additional layer for responders already having to navigate coordination among themselves and the populations they serve.[31] When anyone can participate in both the communications and delivery of aid, how does the mass organize itself, and what is the role of humanitarian organizations in this information ecosystem?

One answer is that it has simply proven very difficult for large traditional organizations and states to play the role of both the information hub and subsequent mobilizer of collective action in humanitarian emergencies. A recent study of the Haiti earthquake found that at the operational level, humanitarian information acquired by the main relief organizations was largely not reinforced by local knowledge. Many governments, national non-governmental organizations, and civil society groups simply started with the assumption that no local data was available. Coordination among these groups was rigid, hierarchical, and cumbersome, leaving them unable to respond to the crisis.[32] A disaster is best thought of as an unpredictable, complex system, yet to create order, large organizations have traditionally imposed a unified, linear, and hierarchical structure, known as a systems model.[33] A complex system is very difficult to impose order on, however, particularly in new digital environments with vast amounts of information arriving in in real time.

And yet new organizations like Ushahidi and OpenStreetMaps are proving very effective in this new context. One way to explain why is by looking to complex adaptive systems theory, which posits that actors in a complex system exist in a constant state of learning, which allows a system as a whole to remain resilient. In a crisis situation, this is important because it allows for behaviors to emerge in the spaces left absent by traditional organizations and structures.[34] So, for example, a group of students outside Boston could fill the information gaps left by a failure of traditional institutions to innovate in the digital space.

———

Crisis mappers are disruptive innovators, and digital humanitarians may be part of a shift in power from states or organizations that used to control aid. Ultimately, however, what matters is whether humanitarian assistance is helping people. Do these digital innovations empower responders and recipients in a way that leads to better outcomes? Or do they simple recreate existing institutional norms, power structures, and social inequities?

Haiti remains in a state of humanitarian emergency, widespread poverty, and deep corruption after years of large-scale international intervention. How then can it be a turning point for humanitarian innovation, as is so often claimed? First, Haiti's history before the earthquake reveals a long-running pattern of "permanent crisis." When the US military restored President Jean-Bertrand Aristide to power in 1994, international relief organizations saw Haiti as an emergency state, a label the country has not been able to shake. This led to INGOs focusing on short-term projects rather than long-term infrastructural development—so that the state was in a sense "de-capacitated" by aid, not improved. The earthquake did a great deal of damage to government buildings and resources—a majority of government buildings were destroyed, and many government employees were killed. However, less than 1% of the $1.8 billion raised for aid went to the Haitian government and restoration of government facilities. Most of the aid was distributed to foreign, non-state actors.

While many of the innovations were attributed to the initial response period, the line between emergency assistance and long-term development is always blurred, particularly in countries with large-scale structural impediments to reconstruction and post-disaster social and economic recovery. As a review of USAID by the NGO Interaction states, "The structure of US assistance still reflects an outmoded dichotomy between 'relief' and 'development' in which effective coordination and handover between these poles is often discussed but rarely executed."[35]

The initial aid effort in Haiti quickly turned into a more traditional development mission, mired in the organizational and government challenges that currently sit largely outside the bounds of technological innovation. For example, agencies run by certified NGOs in Haiti were the main authorities managing camps. They ran on a "project management logic" in which they prioritized meeting NGO goals of delivering a minimum quality of service to those receiving aid. This translated to quantity over quality in terms of the number of people in need served. Additionally, there is remarkably little accountability for individual camp-management agencies. "While failures of quality and coverage within project sites are attributable to specific CMAs, failures of coverage for the whole disaster-affected population are traceable only to the amorphous 'humanitarian system,' where accountability is radically dispersed."[36] Some critics go further in blaming the humanitarian community. Laura Zanotti points out that 84 cents of every dollar USAID spends in Haiti goes to the salaries of international experts.[37]

Another question we must ask then is whether digital technology, despite the benefits outlined previously, has a substantive impact on the core structural challenges of development and humanitarianism. Does it shift power balances in some of the vexing problems we know are rampant in the aid enterprise, such as gender, economic inequality, or culture?

Nigerian anthropologist Gado Alzouma says that "instead of being a tool for liberation, the Internet can become an intimidating technology which can contribute to widening the gap between those who possess everything and those who do not."[38] Despite some promising initiatives that actively engage young women in tech, the introduction of digital technologies often magnifies gender imbalances in developing nations.[39] Women often don't have equal access to education; many societies have ingrained beliefs that technology is a male domain. Knowledge of English, the dominant language of much technology development, is another barrier to involvement in new technologies beyond passive usage. As a result, those who already have power in a society, as well as outsiders, often make coding, design, and infrastructure decisions in the design of humanitarian projects. While code is becoming increasingly powerful, in many ways forming new laws of society, both the government and individual citizens are largely cut out of its creations.

Manuel Castells argues that there is a "fourth world" of people globally who are cut off from larger networks of communication by poverty and lack of infrastructure. He argues that growth of communications technology is a function of globalization and capitalism, and that we must "redefine social development" to include communications technology, or the people in the fourth world will move further into underdevelopment.[40] Within many societies, the access gap exists between urban and rural, rich and poor, men and women, educated and uneducated.[41] Technologies must in part be developed in the environments where they will be used, to incorporate the community dynamics and goals and developmental priorities.[42]

The concept of governing at a distance is often applied to the ways outsiders rule much of a society when responding to a disaster—from the design of camps and the provision of goods and services to more structural controls such as grant giving and project evaluation.[43] In a study of Google Earth's "Crisis in Darfur" Awareness Layer, academic Lisa Parks explores how the presentation of Darfur material can "reproduce western tropes of African tragedy."[44] She argues that instead of leading to policy action, these images have fostered a particular, highly removed and representational version of the events that took place.

Some scholars of geography like Jeffrey Warren warn that we must view mapping as an "inherently un-neutral practice."[45] We must therefore understand its role "not as documentation of what makes up the world but as rhetorical, tactical, and subjective tools." Seen this way, mapping can be a form of control over those who do not participate in the creation of maps.

As Warren points out, digital technology skeptics such as Evgeny Morozov warn that while Brazilian ecologists can use mapping to reveal deforestation policies in the Amazon delta, governments can use these same mapping platforms to monitor and control their citizens. For example, "In Russia, the Internet has given a boost to extreme right-wing groups like the Movement against Illegal Immigration, which has been using Google Maps to visualize the location of ethnic minorities in Russian cities and encouraging its members to hound them out."[46]

The same technology platforms enable these parallel examples of utopian liberation and dystopian control. A crisis map may bring real benefits to those who participate in its creation by providing data. But this data can also be used for harm. If someone in danger is identified and harmed through information on a map, or a woman reporting a rape on HarrassMap is identified and harmed by her abuser, then who is held accountable? If a government uses a crisis map as a source of surveillance data, how do we account for this in an analysis of its utility and value? Accountability in open, collaborative systems is a challenge.

Additionally, the assistance that people receive from participating in a crisis map will in most cases rely on the help of traditional aid organizations. These platforms, while an innovation, are being designed and built by privileged outsiders, who are in very tangible ways benefiting from the deployment of the technology. What's more, they are doing so with the necessary participation of those who are most disenfranchised. We need to be very careful that we are not simply replicating the power structures that have proved so problematic in the wider aid and humanitarian world.

Who is empowered in any given crowdsourced data project? Generally, these are the people who built the platform and analyze the data. They are acquiring knowledge, analytic capability, expertise, and technological advances. Many are becoming experts, and many are employed through this practice. In this sense, many innovations simply mimic the top-down structure that is problematic with many Western-led humanitarian and development projects. For example, Ushahidi maps are usually managed by a small group, likely located in an office away from the area which it maps and gathering information from a large group of affected people. The people who benefit most from this arrangement are those at the top, the ones managing the map: They have the most access to information and face the least risk. However, the data providers on the ground, at the bottom of this structure, may never benefit from reporting what they see.

Those who provide the data required to make the systems work can be empowered by their participation, but only if they see a direct response. And the ability for this to occur is often deeply embroiled in the structural problems that led to their harm in the first place. Delivery of aid still depends on large institutional actors, whether they are national or foreign governments, or international organizations. And while these institutions may engage with the new digital humanitarians, they could also simply appropriate the technology. What's more, when the line between humanitarian assistance and development gets blurred, as is so often the case, then the interplay between individual empowerment through technology and domestic state control and responsibility becomes even more complex. Again, the digital technology cannot be separated from the social system in which it is used, and there are few domains of the international system where this is more consequential than in aid and humanitarianism.

Digital technology may be disrupting aspects of humanitarianism, but is it ultimately helping those doing the saving more than those who remain in need?

CHAPTER SEVEN

DIPLOMACY UNBOUND

At 5 A.M. on Friday, September 7, 2012, five Canadian diplomats stationed in Tehran quietly left Iran. Canada expelled all Iranian diplomats from Ottawa that same day. After years of increasing tensions and rhetoric, and amid growing concerns about possible reprisals from an Israeli or US military strike, Canada cut all diplomatic tries with Iran.

The relationship had soured. The Canadian embassy, which had cost $7 million per year to maintain, had almost no contact with Iranian officials. What was the value to traditional diplomacy, Canadian officials reasoned, if you couldn't talk to anyone? Not everyone agreed with this fairly dramatic piece of statecraft. John Mundy, a veteran Canadian diplomat and the last full Canadian ambassador to Iran, told the *Globe and Mail* that the pullout was a grave step that would be very difficult to repair, and one that precluded Canada from having any dialogue with Iran.[1]

Mundy meant dialogue with the Iranian government. As Canada was cutting its formal diplomatic ties with Iranian officials, a separate team within the Department of Foreign Affairs and International Trade was working

on engaging directly with Iranians. The department partnered with the Munk School of Global Affairs at the University of Toronto, specifically researchers from the Citizen
Lab and ASL19 (a research lab that helps Iranians engage
with surveillance circumvention technology), to form the
Iran Global Dialogue on the Future of Iran and build an
online platform where Iranians could discuss their upcom-
ing election. If Canadian diplomats could not speak to Iranian officials, they were going to help Iranians speak to
one another.

A two-day conference took place in Toronto in May
2013 and was streamed live over the Internet. Its goal
was to provide Iranian democracy activists with a platform to build civil society. Or, more generally, to advance
human rights in Iran. So the conference was held mostly
in Farsi, with translations into English and French, and
people from around the world could participate through
a range of social media platforms, and even email a Canadian "Direct Diplomacy Team." To allow people in
Iran, where there is mass surveillance and censorship of
the Internet, to participate in the conference, the Canadian Department of Foreign Affairs, Trade and Development (DFATD) employed a wide range of circumvention
technologies including Tor and Psiphon, which allow
users to navigate online anonymously and to circumvent government censorship. As of mid-2014, the site
has received more than 4 million unique visitors from
inside Iran, and after Hassan Rouhani won the election,
Global Dialogue launched a follow-up project called the
Rouhani Meter, which measures the Iranian president's

achievements against the promises he made during his campaign.

Many have innocuously characterized the Global Dialogue as the equivalent of a "digital public square," but it is without question aggressive. As Michael Petrou of *Maclean's* magazine reported, one Canadian official acknowledged that the "Iranian government would certainly view such activity on Canada's part as a hostile act, and involvement by its citizens as seditious."[2] While this project might further the Canadian government's goal of fostering civil society, and perhaps even an ancillary objective of fueling dissent in Iran, it comes with costs to Canada's ability to act on the more traditional stage of state-to-state diplomacy.

Foreign Affairs Minister John Baird is sanguine about the trade-off. "We can engage in direct diplomacy, not just elite diplomacy," he said and called for getting more Canadian officials on Twitter. "In the environment of instant communication and social media, we do have to move faster and not be afraid to try new things or to make mistakes." To Baird, the Global Dialogue is only one component of a far more assertive form of diplomacy.

In some ways then, Canada's closure of formal diplomatic channels with Iran and its shift to digital diplomacy does not replace a traditional Canadian role of moderate interlocutor, but rather is an expression of an activist foreign policy. Online, Baird and Prime Minister Stephen Harper were free to call the election a "sham" and to provoke the Iranian government in a way they likely wouldn't have on the ground in Tehran. They were also able to speak directly to millions of Iranians in a way previously impossible.

The US government was also deeply frustrated with the lack of diplomatic progress with Iran. After President Barack Obama's 2009 inauguration, in an effort to reinstate high-level diplomatic discussions, his administration reached out to Iran by contacting the Supreme Leader, Ayatollah Ali Khamenei. Like many previous American overtures, the effort led nowhere.

That summer, Iran detained three American hikers who had attempted to cross the border from Iraq. Oman's Sultan Qaboos initially acted as a mediator between the United States and Iran, leading to the hikers' release and the beginning of backroom discussions between negotiators for the two countries. Top US officials, including Vice President Joe Biden's foreign policy adviser Jake Sullivan, met at least five times with Iranian officials in Oman. These meetings, arranged in secret, with remarkable levels of clandestine movement, were held simultaneously with more public negotiations between Iranian officials and representatives of the United States and its allies. At the last minute, the United States brought a new agreement to the more public table, one developed through these backchannel negotiations with Iran, which none of its allies, not even Israel, knew about. The resulting Geneva agreement provided Iran with $7 billion in sanctions relief in exchange for temporary curbs on nuclear development. The agreement is intended as a first step toward a final accord to be developed in 2015. It is the first major breakthrough in diplomatic relations between Iran and the West in decades, one driven in part by a common perceived interest in confronting the Islamic State of Iraq and Syria (ISIS).

Israeli Prime Minister Benjamin Netanyahu called the deal a historic mistake that "turns the world into a much scarier place," and Canadian Prime Minister Harper also criticized it.[3] But the Geneva agreement is clearly a foreign policy achievement for Obama, who sees an American interest in avoiding the back-and-forth threats that could lead eventually to either US or Israeli military intervention in Iran. It is yet to be seen whether the process will prove a success, but it was a classic diplomatic effort. Not unlike Kissinger's secret trips through Pakistan to meet with Chinese officials, which ultimately led to Nixon's historic visit, these negotiations are rooted in a very traditional notion of diplomacy.

This traditional approach focuses almost exclusively on conversation between elites. High-level talks used to be sufficient, as most relevant groups in a given conflict were essentially hierarchical organizations. Just as diplomats were once the filters for news of global events for their home governments, they were also a primary participant in what was an elites discussion. There was always someone with whom they could, in theory, negotiate. Nelson Mandela was a dissident but also the public representative of a constituency for whom he could speak. Today, diplomats can, and often need to, engage with a wide variety of networked citizens. Like the foreign correspondent in a sea of social media, they are one among many seeking influence as global events unfold. The consequence of failing to adapt will be losing control over the information environment and networks of influencers. This new, net-worked environment challenges what it means to perform diplomacy.

———

To assess whether digital diplomacy can be an effective tool for the state, it is worth stepping back and looking at the place of diplomacy in the projection of state power and the securing of state interests. State diplomacy has, of course, been at the center of international affairs since the Treaty of Westphalia. Epitomized by Otto Von Bismarck's European statecraft through the middle of the 19th century, keeping Europe from war and in so doing building the German Empire, the idea of a balance of power among states, pursued without war, has a long history. It is what underlies the creation of the United Nations following the Second World War and the peace among great powers that it was designed to ensure. Before Twitter and mesh networks and digital security programs, how did we view the value of diplomacy, and how did we evaluate its impact?

Power in the diplomatic context is considered the ability to affect others in order to obtain the outcomes one wants. There are three main ways this can be done. First, coercion is a form of hard power whereby the threat of military force is used as a stick to achieve a political end. Second, inducement and payments are also a form of hard power whereby economic advantages are dangled like a carrot. The third type of diplomatic power is based on attraction rather than confrontation; it is more subtle and is generally called soft power. Other countries may aspire to emulate one country's success or admire its values, and are thus more likely to follow its guidance or policy agenda. The ideal form of soft power is the ability to convince others to want what you want, so that you do not have to force the other to take the action you desire.

As discussed in the second chapter, the idea of soft power is generally attributed to Harvard's Kennedy School of Government professor Joseph Nye, who defines it as "the ability to affect others to obtain the outcomes one wants through attraction rather than coercion or payment." A country's soft power, he argues, "rests on its resources of culture, values, and policies."[4] Soft power is not exactly policy but rather a consequence of policies. Countries can, of course, do things to promote themselves, but this can be risky. If, for example, the Voice of America were to be perceived as arrogant by those it was seeking to influence, Nye explains, then it would not exert soft power.[5] There is a fine line between soft power and propaganda.

Soft power is not a recent American invention. After the Franco-Prussian war, France founded the Alliance Francaise, which has outposts in many countries; and during World War I, many other nations acted in a similar manner, establishing their own cultural offices around the world to develop soft power. In the United States, the idea really took shape in the 1930s, where the Roosevelt administration held the position that "America's security depended on its ability to speak to and to win the support of people in other countries."[6]

Ultimately, soft power is not just getting people to do what they normally wouldn't but also about aligning their interests with your own, often as a result of a long and trusting relationship. This means that the decline or disruption of these relationships can undermine soft power. For example, as Nye outlines, when the United States was seeking support for the Iraq war after the September 11, 2001, attacks, whether it was Mexico's UN vote or the use of Turkish airspace, "the decline of American soft power created a disabling rather than an enabling environment for its policies."[7]

Soft power as an instrument of foreign policy is generally associated with public diplomacy, which may be defined as "the relationship between diplomats and the foreign publics with whom they work." US diplomat Edmund Gullion coined the term in the 1960s, and throughout the Cold War its main concern was promoting US culture worldwide. The projection of American military force and capability, as well as Mikhail Gorbachev's failure to reform his communist government played major roles in ending the Cold War, but so too, argues Nye, did the "soft power of liberal ideas."[8] After the Cold War, budgets were cut and public diplomacy efforts declined, but 9/11 and the War on Terror made it all the more important for the United States to assert its cultural values around the world.

Public diplomacy has traditionally taken three forms: explaining government foreign policies to those impacted by them, developing long-term strategic themes to brand foreign policy, and building lasting relationships through cultural and academic exchanges. Notably, in the past, public diplomacy has not made policy, but rather has communicated and framed it. But this is changing, as the practice moves into the digital space.

Despite this clear mandate, the place of both soft power and public diplomacy in the broader diplomatic landscape is increasingly ambiguous. Jan Melissen, professor of diplomacy at the Netherlands Institute for International Affairs argues, that "the basic distinction between traditional diplomacy and public diplomacy is clear: the former is about relationships between the representatives of states, or other international actors; whereas the latter targets the general public in foreign societies and more specific non-official groups, organizations and individuals."[9] In a networked world, the audience for public diplomacy initiatives is increasingly vast and hard to define. At times, it seems as if digital public diplomacy means relations with anyone and everyone.

———

President Barack Obama's major address in Cairo on June 4, 2009, was an attempt to "reframe the relationship between the US and the Muslim world." As the first major foreign policy initiative of his presidency, Obama sought to shift the public discourse and perception in the Middle East about America and American foreign policy that had so soured under his predecessor, George W. Bush, in the wake of the Iraq War. Ten years earlier, Obama might have taking to the airwaves and opinion pages of newspapers to promote this message. In 2009 it meant engaging the online world.

For this task Obama deployed the State Department's Digital Outreach Team, a pioneer in digital diplomacy. The Digital Outreach Team is a small group of State Department officials who engage in foreign comment threads and online forums in order to "counter misinformation." The team visits popular Arabic, Farsi, and Urdu news websites with large pools of commenters. Members identify themselves by name and acknowledge their affiliation with the Department of State. American public diplomacy is certainly not new to the Middle East, but it once took a very different form. Up until the mid-1990s, diplomatic efforts were run by the United States Information Agency, which used the Voice of America to broadcast in Arabic and produced an Arabic magazine called *Al-Majal*. During the Gulf War, the State Department developed new radio stations, as well as a television station called Al-Hurra. Neither was particularly successful and both lacked credibility in the Arab world.[10] Unlike previous efforts—magazines, radio, and television that broadcast American views to an Arab audience—the Digital Outreach Team took up active, constant, real-time engagement.

So when Obama courted Arab and Muslim audiences around his Cairo speech, he was entering uncharted and perilous territory. An academic study of the Digital Outreach Team's efforts looked at how American messages were received on discussion boards and news sites in the Middle East. The authors found that the team primarily worked to dispel myths about US policy and refute false claims, but at times they came off as condescending or ridiculing. The study also found that posts by the Digital Outreach Team generated more negative response toward the United States than had already been posted, and these reactions were so strong that American engagement seemed ultimately counterproductive. Comment threads are notoriously irascible places, and they may not be the best platform for diplomacy. In any case, the Digital Outreach Team has explained that their primary goal is to present logical and informed arguments to counter anti-US sentiment online, not for the commenters, who make up a fraction of the online audience, but for the broader, silent audience that gets their news from these sites.[11]

Digital public diplomacy has seen wide international adoption. Ambassadors and desk officers use Twitter to engage their home constituents or citizens of the countries where they are posted. Foreign ministers hold online briefings on Facebook, Twitter, and Google Hangouts, and events are streamed online. As the State Department writes, "The role of new media in public diplomacy has gone from virtually non-existent to standard practice." Indeed, in the summer of 2014, the Department had 230 Facebook pages, 80 Twitter accounts, 55 channels on YouTube, and 40 accounts on Flickr. In the US State Department, many such initiatives fall under the Bureau of Information Resource Management's Office of eDiplomacy.

The department has also used technology to change its own internal processes. The Communities@State project allows department staff to form online communities, start blogs, and discuss policy, with the goal of breaking down departmental silos and fostering better internal communication. Diplopedia is an internal wiki where officials can create articles that others can edit collaboratively. One of the main advantages of this site is helping with the continuity of programs once offices are moved to other desks— it is a place where past knowledge can be stored. Virtual Presence Posts is a suite of online tools to help consulates and embassies better engage with the public. This is particularly useful in countries where the United States has no physical presence.[12]

Digitizing the traditional tools of public diplomacy is both appropriate and needed. Doing so is more complex than old broadcast models because one has to both communicate and actively engage, but ultimately this is doable and will prove beneficial to the promotion of state interests.

The challenge any public diplomacy initiative faces is that it does not exist in a vacuum. As such, it must be assessed alongside a much broader range of, at times, contradicting or conflicting policies. Just as Nixon's diplomatic overtures to China were not exogenous from the actions of other branches of US foreign policy, Canada's digital outreach to Iranian activists should not be viewed as independent from that country's strenuous objections to the US-led treaty process. The Iranians whom Canada were seeking to engage in a conversation about their human rights were aware of Canada's opposition to a nuclear deal on which their economic prosperity and re-engagement with the international community depended.

This is why US outreach to the Arab world during the Iraq War should not be seen as a failure of public diplomacy, but as a function of how people felt and were affected by the war. And Obama's attempted digital reparations were dismissed by many in the region not due to the medium in which they were debated but because of deep-seated skepticism after years of perceived antagonism.

As the Digital Outreach Team found in its efforts around Obama's Cairo speech, the greatest hindrance to the online effort was US foreign policy in the Middle East itself. "The work of the Digital Outreach Team is being undermined by the trajectory of US foreign policy towards the Middle East," they pointedly concluded.[13] No amount of tweeting will make a difference if the message being sold is unappealing.

As many of the State Department's digital public diplomacy initiatives took off, the department was developing a broader array of digital programs. Fitting under this evolving rubric of 21st-century statecraft are many programs that extended far beyond the use of Twitter and force us to consider the bounds and ultimate costs of more activist online diplomacy.

As Secretary of State Hillary Clinton said, they were "working to leverage the power and potential in what I call 21st-Century Statecraft . . . to embrace new tools, like using cell phones for mobile banking or to monitor elections. But we're also reaching to the people behind these tools, the innovators and entrepreneurs themselves."

The 21st-century statecraft policy framework came out of the First Quadrennial Diplomacy and Development Review in 2010, which outlined the wide range of new actors, technologies, and platforms that needed to be incorporated into US diplomatic policy—not simply in the promotion of government policy but also in the creation and implementation of it. As has been outlined throughout this book, these actors are powerful and their capabilities often confound states. Extending US diplomacy into this space means engaging on platforms where participants are anonymous, deploying technologies that are widely used by criminal organizations, and actively incorporating actors whom the government generally dismisses (such as Anonymous and Telecomix) into the conversation of diplomacy.

Officially, the department defines 21st-century statecraft as "the complementing of traditional foreign policy tools with newly innovated and adapted instruments of statecraft that fully leverages the networks, technologies, and demographics of our interconnected world." Pointedly, they argue that "these new forms of decentralized power reflect fundamental shifts in the structure of information systems in modern societies."

A broad range of development, policy, and public-diplomacy programs falls under this framework. The Civil Society 2.0 project is essentially a tech training camp for NGOs and civil society organizations around the world. The State Department sends American technologists abroad to hold two-day training workshops to help these organizations improve their reach and impact. Tech@State brings together American technologists, government personnel, and partner organizations to brainstorm and develop technology-based solutions for problems falling under the targeted goals of the US diplomacy and development agenda, such as education, health care, and poverty alleviation. The Developer Community is a site for APIs (application programming interface), RSS (rich site summary) feeds, and government databases that can encourage developers to create applications.

Other programs address the shift in the power balances laid out in the Diplomacy and Development Review. The Internet in a Suitcase, supplied to Syrian rebels through the Office of Syrian Opposition Support as part of $25 million in non-lethal aid, is a collaboration with several US non-profit partners to develop mesh network technology so communities of activists can communicate securely during communications blackouts and provide digital security for network operators and users.[14] Another project was a joint State Department and Pentagon attempt to circumvent Taliban control of communication services by creating an independent cellphone network using towers on military bases.[15] To function effectively, these so-called dissent networks need to be highly secure and to be able to connect a large number of people across a significant distance.[16] Shadi Hasan wrote an electrical engineering and computer science thesis on designing networks that can function in large-scale Internet blackouts, and he argues that achieving these at the same time is a core challenge of the community of technologists and activists developing censorship circumvention capabilities; "true dissent network would fundamentally change the balance of power between repressive regimes and dissidents in terms of access to communication."[17]

Such programs are being deployed in spaces of active conflict. The State Department, for example, has supplied $25 million in counter-surveillance technology to Syrian rebels through the Office of Syrian Opposition Support.

This technology mostly came in the form of satellite phones. A similar joint State Department and Pentagon project attempts to circumvent Taliban control of communication services by creating an independent cellphone network using towers on military bases.

Another more activist digital diplomacy effort was an elaborate scheme to create a Cuban version of Twitter with the goal of fostering dissent and promoting regime change there. Between 2009 and 2012, USAID, the international development arm of the State Department responsible for a wide range of humanitarian and aid projects around the world, developed a mobile text-based service through a clandestine network of contractors and front companies allowing Cubans to freely exchange information. The service, called ZunZuneo, had 40,000 active users at its peak. When it attempted to transition to a private company, it failed to find a sustainable revenue model.

The program was ingenious, audacious—and ultimately a stain on the reputation of USAID, known for a wide range of benign development projects. As Republican Senator Mike Johanns said at a hearing into the matter, "When I think about USAID I think about words like 'humanitarian,' 'caring,' 'road builders.' I can't imagine why USAID would want to be involved in something like going into a country and trying to get Internet access for people opposing the regime."

This is of course not entirely true. The USAID has a long history of interventionist development initiatives. For example, since the mid-2000s, the US has been spending tens of millions of dollars a year on what they call "transformational development" initiatives in Iran.

————

Both the mesh network initiative and the USAID Cuban project are attempts by the state to act as a disruptive power itself. The core challenge of the State Department's Internet freedom agenda is not that circumvention tools are a bad idea, or that the censorship and surveillance programs they are meant to counter are not damaging to civil society. It is that at the same time as the 21st-century statecraft program was supplying Syrian dissidents with counter-surveillance technology the US government was simultaneously building a large-scale international surveillance program of its own. What's more, at the same time the United States was supporting these dissidents to oppose certain regimes, the regimes were often buying their surveillance hardware from American corporations, at the same technology trade fairs as the US intelligence agencies. It is an understatement to say that activists will be suspicious of US efforts going forward. No matter how genuine the intentions, the State Department's Internet freedom agenda cannot be isolated from the wider actions of the US government.

This dynamic can work in the other direction as well. Digital diplomacy initiatives can negate the efforts of other branches of foreign policy. For example, the Cuban social network, while an innovative use of digital technology to achieve a (however misguided) State Department objective, tainted the reputation and hurt the effectiveness of USAID as a whole. In Cuba, it fed directly into a narrative of US malfeasance and ended the other good works being done by the Cuba-based USAID project. Globally, it put USAID personnel at risk and marginalized their capability to deliver on their often very worthy humanitarian objectives.

And this gets to the core challenge of digital diplomacy, one that stems from the shift in medium represented by digital technology. It is not just a shift in communication platforms to which the practice of diplomacy must adjust. The Internet and digital networks are a new space of operation entirely, with their own power structures, actors, and norms of behavior. Yes, digital public diplomacy initiatives can increase the reach of the state's message, and taking to Twitter will help diplomats engage with local populations. But when the state truly embraced digital tools and capabilities, the resulting innovative digital diplomacy projects, the ones that actually have the potential to shift the state into this new space of operation, were the ones that ultimately failed. They failed because the state operates under different social, legal, and at times, ethical constraints from other online actors. And the costs of operating outside of these bounds, taken with the state's foreign policy interests as a whole, are simply too high. While traditional state-to-state diplomacy will always be relevant, it might be that diplomatic power, or soft power, does not translate to the digital world.

It is notable, for example, that Anne-Marie Slaughter, whose theory of networked power was detailed in Chapter 2, was director of policy planning (a highly influential policy position) at the State Department while the

21st-century statecraft policy was being developed. She has rightly argued that the state needs to engage in this new digital space and is only one actor of many. She does so in a way, however, that ultimately privileges the state. Both Slaughter and Nye believe that the interests of the United States and of the networked actors they seek to influence can be made compatible. The state just has to behave in a way that is relevant to the digital world. But the case of digital diplomacy shows that this theory has limitations.

When the bounds of diplomacy are extended into influencing not just states but also digital actors, then they overlap fundamentally with other foreign policy programs and objectives. And this invariably leads to conflicting methods and outcomes. Because these more invasive digital diplomacy initiatives are implemented on the very same platforms and using the same tools as the more innocuous digital public diplomacy programs, it is possible that they tarnish the whole enterprise. If this is the case, then the undue negative costs associated with coercive digital diplomacy demonstrate the weakness of the state in a major realm of its foreign policy. And if the state can't effectively act diplomatically in the digital space, then what does this tell us about the contemporary relevance of diplomacy itself?

Returning to the competing approaches to Iranian diplomacy, if the goal was to influence the Iranian state to limit their nuclear production, then the US model has for now been effective. It is a traditional diplomatic goal, which fits comfortably within the purview and capability of the State Department. The Canadian program has stepped out into a far more ambiguous space. While there is no question that it met its goal of reaching out to Iranian citizens, if it was an attempt to influence the Iranian government by building civil society and perhaps fostering dissent, then we need to question the capabilities of the Canadian state to see this through. We have to take into consideration the wide ranges of implications for doing this, and we are far from knowing the outcome. As an initiative it may have been successfully, but it must be seen, and ultimately assessed, as a part of a wider foreign policy.

If, on the other hand, this is the Canadian state deciding that the traditional goals of diplomacy (in this case, influencing the Iranian government) are obsolete, then they will run into a whole different set of challenges. When diplomacy steps out of the bounds of the state system and into the digital world, it has to play in the game that is being played. And as we have seen throughout this book, in this space the rules, norms, and capabilities are very different. As we have seen in the 21st-century statecraft examples, the state is profoundly ill-suited to behave in this way, without taking significant risks that will affect a wide range of other foreign policy goals.

Ultimately, the challenge of digital diplomacy is grounded in the paradox of state power online, that states either can't do the things necessary to exert power in a digital network or the strategic costs of doing so are simply too high. What's more, the goals, tools, and strategic frameworks through which this form of invasive digital diplomacy needs to operate extend the bounds of diplomacy so far and overlap so significantly with other foreign policy goals that they render the practices of diplomacy obsolete.

CHAPTER EIGHT

THE VIOLENCE
OF ALGORITHMS

In December 2010, I attended a training session in Tysons Corner, Virginia, just outside Washington, DC, for an intelligence analytics software program called Palantir. Co-founded by Peter Thiel, a libertarian Silicon Valley billionaire from PayPal and Facebook, Palantir is a slick tool kit of data visualization and analytics used by the NSA, FBI, CIA, and other US national security and policing institutions. As far as I could tell, I was the only civilian in the course, which I took to explore Palantir's potential for use in academic research.

Palantir is designed to pull together as much data as possible, then tag it and try to make sense of it. For example, all of the data about a military area of operation, including base maps, daily intelligence reports, mission reports, and the massive amounts of surveillance data now being collected could be viewed and analyzed for patterns in one platform. The vision being sold is one of total comprehension, of making sense of a messy operating environment flooded with data. The company has a Silicon Valley mentality: War is hell. Palantir can cut through the fog.

The Palantir trainer took us through a demonstration "investigation." Each trainee got a workstation with two screens and various datasets: a list of known insurgents, daily intelligence reports, satellite surveillance data, and detailed city maps. We uploaded these into Palantir, one by one, and each new dataset showed us a new analytic capability of the program. With more data came greater clarity—which is not what usually happens when an analyst is presented with vast streams of data.

In our final exercise, we added information about the itinerary of a suspected insurgent, and Palantir correlated the location and time of one meeting with information it had about the movements of a known bombmaker. In "real life," the next step would be a military operation: the launch of a drone strike, the deployment of a Special Forces team. Palantir had shown us how an analyst could process disparate data sources efficiently to target the use of violence. It was an impressive demonstration, and probably an easy sell for the government analysts taking the course.

But I left Tysons Corner with plenty of questions. The data we input and tagged included typos and other mistakes, as well as our unconscious biases. When we marked an individual as a suspect, that data was pulled into the Palantir database as a discrete piece of information, to be viewed and analyzed by anyone with access to the system, decontextualized from the rationale behind our assessment. Palantir's algorithms—the conclusions and recommendations that make its system "useful"—carry the biases and errors of the people who wrote them. For example, the suspected insurgent might have turned up in multiple intelligence reports, one calling him a possible threat and another that provided a more nuanced assessment of him. When the suspected insurgent is then cross-referenced with a known bombmaker, you can bet which analysis was prioritized. Such questions have not slowed down Palantir, which developed a billion-dollar valuation faster than any other American company before it, largely due to its government security contracts. In 2014 Palantir's value was between $5 billion and $8 billion dollars.

And analysts who use it have no shortage of data to feed into the system. All around us sensors are collecting data at a scale and with a precision that in many cases is nearing real-time total surveillance. For example, wide-area surveillance, also called persistent ground surveillance systems, which local law-enforcement agencies use, create networks of video cameras to detect and analyze crime in near real time.[1] Newer wide-area surveillance systems do not require a network of individual cameras but can instead take high-resolution images of many square miles at once. The Department of Homeland Security tethered such a motion-imagery system 2,000 feet above the desert in Nogales, Arizona. On its first night in use, the system identified 30 suspects who were brought in for questioning.[2]

This type of video analysis requires new image-processing capabilities. The MATE system, for example, detects movement in the camera's field of vision that the human eye, even a trained officer, would not notice; this can be used in airports to detect a suspicious bag. The Camero Xaver system uses 3D image reconstruction algorithms and ultra-wideband (UWB) sensors to create representations of objects behind barriers.[3] In other words, it can see through walls.

Facial recognition and other biometrics technology are also progressing rapidly. A pilot program in San Diego called the Automated Regional Justice Information System applies algorithms to individual frames from live video feeds and then can cross-reference a face against pictures in databases at a rate of a million comparisons a second.[4] One of the founders of facial recognition technology, physicist Joseph J. Atick, is now cautioning against its proliferation, arguing that it is "basically robbing everyone of their anonymity." A company called Extreme Reality has developed a biometric scanning system that takes images from surveillance video to create a map of a person's skeleton and uses it as a baseline for detecting suspicious movements.[5] Google Glass and other miniature cameras move us toward a world in which nothing is private, and all behavior is captured.

It's not enough to collect all this data, and there are limits on the processing power that allows computers to make sense of it. But if research on quantum computing continues to progress at its current pace, those limits could disappear.[6] For political theorist James Der Derian, this potential revolutionary advance in computational capability has dramatic implications for the international order. Whoever has access to quantum computing power will have such an advantage over the control and understanding of information that it could lead to a new kind of arms race. Those who possess quantum computers could in theory predict the stock market, model global weather patterns, make significant advances in artificial intelligence, and have the ability to process and understand vast stores of real-time surveillance data.

As Der Derian argues, this could signal a new age and form of war. "The goal is to convey a verbal facsimile of contemporary global violence as it phase-shifts from a classically scripted War 1.0 to an image-based War 2.0, to an indeterminate, probabilistic and observable-dependent form that defies fixation by word, number or image, that is, quantum war."[7] Philosopher Paul Virilio warns of the potential for a future "information bomb" where disaster can occur simultaneously, everywhere on the planet. This is a concept acknowledged in theoretical physics but not in the social sciences. It is for this reason that Der Derian urges an integration of science and math into the study of international relations. He explains that disciplinary borders must be eliminated in favor of a "post classical approach," one that moves away from the traditional linear and systematic understanding of war, to one that accounts for its messiness and non-linearity.

The potential power of quantum computing puts information control at the center of warfare. Andrew Marshall, director of the Office of Net Assessment, US Department of Defense, has said, if World War I was the chemists' war, and World War II was the physicists' war, World War III will be the information researchers' war.

————

Over the course of history, the automation of military technology has put more distance between the soldier and his target. Crossbows, muskets, machine guns, and airplanes put more distance than previous technologies, but they still required human operation and decision making. Increasingly, however, the decisions made in battle are also being automated, eliminating a step of human involvement between analysis and action.

The idea of robotic war, and the protection that it promises, is nothing new. In 1495 Leonardo da Vinci proposed a "mechanical knight" made up of pulleys under a suit of armor. In 1898, Nikola Tesla built a remote-controlled boat that he tried to sell to the US military as an early form of torpedo, an idea that was implemented by the Germans in World War I. The United States first developed a gyroscope-guided bomb in 1914. Throughout the 20th century, most advances in autonomous weaponry involved missile guidance systems. In the 1950s and 1960s, both the Soviet Union and the United States began developing computer guided missiles that correct their flight autonomously. In 1978, the United States deployed the first GPS satellite, inaugurating a system that would greatly enhance the capabilities of unmanned aerial vehicles. These systems are not infallible, however; in 1988, an automated aircraft-defense system on a US battleship in the Persian Gulf mistakenly shot down a commercial airliner, killing 290 people.

But it was only at the turn of the 21st century, with advances in drone technology and artificial intelligence, that the possibilities of robot war began to be realized. The United States has deployed 65 Lockheed Martin blimps in Afghanistan that provide real-time surveillance and data processing across 100 square kilometers at a time.[8] These blimps are equipped with high definition cameras and sensors that detect sound and motion. The 360-degree Kestrel motion-imagery system, for example, can record all activity taking place in a city for periods of up to 30 days. To process all that information, the system only records activity that it assesses as being valuable, and its judgment evolves over time though machine learning.

The United States is not the only country using automated technology. Russia deployed armed robots to guard five ballistic missile installations. Each robot weighs nearly a ton. They can travel at speeds of 45 kilometers per hour, using radar and a laser rangefinder to navigate, analyze potential targets, and fire machine guns without a human pulling the trigger. Russia is planning on vastly increasing its use of armed robots, supposedly saving its military more than a billion dollars a year.[9] South Korea's Super Aegis 2 automated gun tower can lock onto a human target up to three kilometers away in complete darkness and automatically fire a machine gun, rocket launcher, or surface-to-air missile.[10] For now, a human is required to make the final kill decision, but this is not technically required. South Korea has proposed deploying the Super Aegis 2 in the volatile demilitarized zone that separates it from North Korea. Communications between the South and North are terrible, making this move toward automatic killing in the demilitarized zone extremely dangerous. Automation is also used for defensive purposes. The Israeli Iron Dome is an air-defense system designed to shoot down rockets and artillery shells. Israeli officials claim that the Iron Dome, operational since March 2011, shot down more than 400 missiles in its first

18 months. Drones, from the surveillance blimps described, to swarms of microdrones outfitted with cameras and other sensors, represent another major advance that potentially transforms the way military intelligence is collected and processed.

Underlying all of these technologies is computational power. With algorithmic technologies that trace and record movements of people (at airports, through credit card data, our passports, and visual or data surveillance technologies) we can detect patterns and ascribe risk to behaviors outside the "norm." The calibration of this norm can either be a human decision or a computational one, but in the end these norms are built into algorithms. Automation also offers the promise of predicting future events. As machines learn and algorithms develop, this process becomes further and further removed from our human intervention.

This distancing dilutes the responsibility of humans by acting through technologies. As surveillance expert Bruce Schneier notes, "any time we're judged by algorithms, there's the potential for false positive. . . . [O]ur credit ratings depend on algorithms; how we're treated at airport security does, too." And most alarming of all, drone targeting is partly based on algorithmic surveillance.[11] Fully automated drones that can make decisions and even kill by themselves are still in development stages, but they are being actively tested.

As articulated in a 2014 Human Rights Watch report on automated war, "Fully autonomous weapons represent the step beyond remote-controlled armed drones. Unlike any existing weapons, these robots would identify and fire on targets without meaningful human intervention.

They would therefore have the power to determine when to take human life."[12] The international community is taking notice. In the past two years, numerous academic and policy reports have addressed the legal, ethical, and human-rights implications of automated killing, and at the 2014 UN Convention on Certain Conventional Weapons (CCW) conference, automated war was a topic of debate. A civil society campaign has been launched, called the Campaign to Stop Killer Robots.

———

Automation has radically reshaped the geography of violence. Just like Anonymous can wield power without occupying a discrete and contiguous geographical space, states can wage war without invading enemy territory. In practice, this has meant that the difference between international and domestic security paradigms has eroded. While the technology underpinning this capacity was already long in development, the defining moment in this shift was 9/11. The decentralized network of al-Qaeda attacked the heart of a global superpower on the other side of the world.

In response, the United States deviated from both domestic and international legal and military norms in pursuit of a diffuse organization. At home, the Bush administration began to operate under what they called the "one percent doctrine," which dictates that if there is a 1% chance of an event occurring, the government must treat it as a certainty. This doctrine, combined with the questionable notion that 9/11 could have been predicted with proper data, has led to a culture of massive data collection, from the NSA sur-veillance apparatus exposed by Edward Snowden to the widespread deployment of cameras, sensors, and drones. These programs seek to conquer the unknown and, like the promise of Palantir, create order from uncertainty. As geographer Louise Amoore argues, the law shifted to allow and accept the use of massive, invasive databases to monitor the civilian populations for the purpose of "risk management," despite the potential to violate civil rights.[13]

A natural place to introduce these new technologies was on the borders. This new approach to border surveillance began with the Automated Targeting System which assigned risk scores to imported goods as they arrived to US ports in shipping containers on cargo vessels. This system was then applied to people crossing the US border, using an array of data such as financial records, past travel, known move-ment and addresses, race and religion in order to assign risk instantly.[14] This technology replaced with a mathe-matical formula the decisions once made by immigration officers. In 2005, the UK Home Office and US Transporta-tion Security Administration (TSA) started using full body scanners at airports, and movement analysis cameras are being deployed throughout airport terminals, adding new layers of biometric data to the mix.

This spatial blurring has legal implications. The inter-national legal theorist Wouter Werner looks at US and Israeli security policy since 9/11 and argues that acts of war have become less defined and boundless. Werner notes that states are reluctant to declare war yet often give violent and targeted directives that could be seen as warfare. Werner relies on the theories of German political scientist Carl Schmitt, who explored the concept of *justus hostis* or the "just enemy," an aspect of European international order dating from the 16th century. *Justus hostis* is based on the idea of an equal or respectable enemy, one that has similar capacity for fighting and similar standing in the international order as its opponent, the recognition of which was the beginning of international law. This, of course, mostly applies to wars between states. Schmitt argues that the idea of *justis hostis*, however, is in decline with the advent of globalization and new technologies that open up new spaces for war. "To war on both sides belongs a certain chance, a minimum of possibility for victory. Once that ceases to be the case, the opponent becomes nothing more than an object of violent measures. The victors consider their superiority in weaponry to be an indication of their *justa causa*, and declare the enemy to be criminal, because it is no longer possible to realize the concept of *justus hostis*."[15]

Werner argues that the rise of "targeted killing" also blurs the legal definitions of war. In 2006 the Israeli High Court of Justice recognized targeted strikes on individuals as legal, despite protests from human rights groups. The United States has created new categories of "unlawful combatants"; it also argued that the "war on terror" was fundamentally different from other wars, and that enemies did not deserve the same protections. Some scholars compare this language to that used in the 19th century, with reference to "savage warriors," who were thought of as so fundamentally different and outside of the international system that protections given them were simply a choice and not a requirement on the part of the warring state.[16]

Werner is arguing that the bounds of war have been stretched by forces of globalization, by the changing nature of what constitutes an enemy in a post-9/11 conflict, and by new technological capabilities. Both the law and the theoretical principles that underlie our conception of just war are being expanded uncomfortably to fit this new reality.

With the blurring of national and international definitions comes an extension of the tools and practices of war to the domestic context. Tools developed for the battlefield are now being widely applied in domestic contexts, beginning with the US border with Mexico. For 25 miles inside the border, the US Customs and Border Patrol has the legal right to enter anyone's property (including a computer or cell phone) without a warrant.[17] What does it mean when the state extends military technologies and tactics beyond the battlefield? Put another way, what do computational power and surveillance-based weaponry do to the line between war and peace?

The border is fast becoming a testing ground of the US surveillance state: hidden cameras, drones, and 24/7 electronic monitoring, much of it automated. And in an extensive multi-year investigation into the US national intelligence and counterterrorism infrastructure built since 9/11, the *Washington Post* found an almost unimaginably vast national security apparatus. The investigation, called Top-Secret America, found that

1,271 government organizations and 1,931 private companies work on programs related to counterterrorism, homeland security and intelligence in about 10,000 locations across the United States; an estimated 854,000 people, nearly 1.5 times as many people as live in Washington, D.C., hold top-secret security clearances; in Washington and the surrounding area, 33 building complexes for top-secret intelligence work are under construction or have been built since September 2001 which together occupy the equivalent of almost three Pentagons or 22 U.S. Capitol buildings—about 17 million square feet of space; 51 federal organizations and military commands, operating in 15 U.S. cities, track the flow of money to and from terrorist networks; and analysts who make sense of documents and conversations obtained by foreign and domestic spying share their judgment by publishing 50,000 intelligence reports each year.[18]

The reach of this security apparatus is vast, and the amount of money, people, and resources implicated in it is remarkable. The US intelligence budget alone is $75 billion a year, which is a fraction of the entire enterprise. The threat is ill-defined but omnipresent. The battlefield is global. The laws regulating and checking this immense capability are poorly defined and often secret. And the lines between the domestic and the international, whether it be through the sharing of technology and data, or the overlapping of operational theaters, are increasingly blurred. It is safe to say that there is a risk of the United States becoming a national security state.

If this happens, it will be as a reaction to the disruptive powers outlined throughout this book. As new actors are empowered to act in a digital environment in a way that destabilizes and at times confounds the state, whether they are activists, humanitarians, journalists, or terrorists, the state can fight back by seeking to control the network. They will either have to control everything or will have to come to some sort of accommodation with these new disruptive powers. What we currently know about the US surveillance state, and the technological, military, and prosecutorial powers it seems willing to deploy, suggests that the United States at least is seeking the former.

———

If we are indeed heading into an information research war, a Third World War, then it will be because the digital landscape is being weaponized. Take Google Earth, discussed earlier in the context of humanitarianism. The digital mapping of the earth's surface is also a remarkably powerful tool for a wide range of military uses and is increasingly being used as a targeting tool by both states and individuals. A civilian in Germany discovered a Chinese training camp on the China-India border using Google Earth; Russia and South Korea have both requested that Google blur out "sensitive areas"; and India has voiced concerns that public maps could further incite tensions in Kashmir. In the United States, Dick Cheney's house and the Pepsi headquarters are both pixilated out. As the Russian Federal Security Service proclaimed, "Terrorists don't need to reconnoiter their target. Now an American company is working for them."[19]

Cultural historian Bruce Franklin outlines how each era of war has its own "visual style." Vietnam had a guerrilla style, created by embedded journalists shooting rough video on the ground. Then came a cockpit view during the first Gulf War, that showed never before seen images of missile strikes, displaying surreal (and highly misleading) accuracy. Franklin points out that we are now in a period of sanitized drone views. What's more, the gun and the camera are interconnected. Drones are at once a "war machine" and also a "watching machine" that grows more sophisticated with each technological generation and is able to collect and process more and more data. What is unique about this new form of war is that the machines are controlled from the other side of the world, via images themselves. Drones are operated in much the same way as video games—reality controlled by the virtual.[20]

Another important consequence of the de-spatialization of war is in the very conception of security itself, in particular, how we identify what is and is not a security issue, and subsequently how we frame our approach to such issues through the words, as well as images and video, presented to us by government and media.

The idea of "securitization" in international relations theory hinges on the notion that through its rhetoric, the state has the power to identify which topics should be treated as security issues. And this has tremendous consequences. It both raises the perceived importance of an issue and predisposes it to be addressed with militarized solutions. In the 1990s, for example, the US "securitiza-tion" of Africa led to the deployment of a new regional command called AFRICOM.

Following this framing, the Internet, and digital technol-ogy itself, is at risk of being "securitized," and as a con-sequence, being absorbed into the fabric of state military policy. Once an enemy or threat is perceived and labeled in an online ecosystem, the platform or technologies them-selves become the objects of security. This brings with it the discourse, resources, and imperatives of war.[21] An example of this in practice is when the United States identifies users of TOR anonymizing software as potential threats and sub-jects for surveillance, or for the FBI to label the use of mesh networking technology as an indicator of terrorist activity.

Prominent scholar Barry Buzan describes the distin-guishing feature of "securitization" as a specific rhe-torical structure that elevates an issue above politics to the realm of existential crisis. "In security discourse" he argues, "an issue is dramatized and presented as an issue of supreme priority; thus by labeling it as a security issue an agent claims a need for and a right to treat it by ex-traordinary means."[22]

Central to this act of dramatization are images and videos. In the case of the modern security state, this means both the images of violence that are presented to propagate a threat and the underlying importance of image analysts and spatial data processing to the act of conducting actual security operations.

It is useful to think of this as a shift in media, in respect to both issue framing and to state security responses. We must look beyond the state's use of security rhetoric and into how society as a whole is propagating a particular narrative of security via the media. This does not mean that traditional security institutions are losing power; rather, it indicates that the diffusion of the security narrative among actors with different imperatives is critical to understanding the way a culture sees threats and supports particular responses to them.[23]

This cultural view has enabled the state to treat the telecommunications infrastructure in its entirety and all of the participants in it as a security issue. It facilitates the merging of international war and domestic security, and makes the distinction between digital acts and their physical violent manifestations far more difficult to draw.

The act of making the digital world both a threat and a weapon has allowed the state to treat it as an object of war, and has blurred the lines between belligerents and citizens. Coupled with the power that is derived by the state's increasing sophistication in this space—whether through automation, biometrics, or the new forms of social control and the violence they enable—there is reason to question the narrative of empowerment that has been explored throughout this book.

———

For now, automated violence technologies require the power of the state. To do large-scale visual surveillance, for example, one needs both sophisticated sensor deployment platforms and significant computational power. While both are increasingly available in some forms to individuals and groups, supercomputers, quantum computing, militarized drones, and automated weaponry are still very much the purview of the state.

These technologies can be disrupted, however. There have been a few instances of groups hacking into drone computers as well as potential hacks to thwart biometric facial recognition programs. A community of drone operators post videos of drone strikes on YouTube and report on the lives of drone operators—how they can commit acts of war from miles away, and then go "home to eat dinner with their families."

And other states have found ways of fighting back. In 2013 Iranian officials claimed to have hacked a US drone, forced it to land, and recreated some of its technology. The BBC reported that Iranian officials were parading around a downed but unscathed RQ-170 Sentinel stealth drone, known to be used by the CIA. The Iranians claimed that they had not shot it down but had intercepted its GPS software to confuse the drone and force it to land.[24] The United States denied the hack, claiming that the drone's software malfunctioned. Pakistan claims that it also learned how to intercept drones after examining the helicopter that was downed in the raid to capture Osama bin Laden.[25] The *Wall Street Journal* reports that Iraqi insurgents have managed to hack US drones with widely available $25 software, which they used to access video feeds from the drones.[26]

While there are no recorded instances of biometric software being hacked, researchers have found flaws in the programming of facial recognition software that let someone confuse the program with fake photos.[27] There

DISRUPTIVE POWER

have been several reports online of civilians who have been able to hack into security surveillance camera footage.[28] A designer has developed "anti-drone" clothing that thwarts a drone's heat-seeking radar.[29] The same designer is also developing forms of makeup that distort facial features so as to confuse facial recognition software.[30]

While some of these technologies could empower non-state actors—and the civilian capacity in this space will invariably increase with time—there are several reasons the state is likely to continue to dominate the use of algorithmic violence. The entrenchment of the emerging national security state keeps citizens in a state of fear. This means that subjects of surveillance often feel they are being protected by technologies that identify "threats." There is also a very high cost to challenging national security programs. The fear of disproportionate penalties surely dissuades disruptors in this space.

Technological barriers also exist. Many automated technologies require a level of technical capacity, computational power, and data supply that are mainly accessible only by states. Even companies with massive computational capacity, like Google, often bend to the will of the state when it comes to national security. This creates an asymmetry between states and individuals, as well as between powerful and weak states. As technology spreads down to weaker states and individuals, awesome new technologies will likely remain state dominated.

What does the future hold for cyber weaponry? Author Daniel Suarez argues that because these computational, automated tools concentrate tremendous power, they are a harbinger of a recentralization of power and a reversal of a five-century-old trend to greater democracy. Remote force deployment of instruments such as microdrones could theoretically allow the state to kill anonymously. Combined with machine learning and artificial intelligence, powers could target dissidents before they gain traction. This is a path to anonymous war.

The obvious solution to this theoretical dystopia, Suarez argues, is to ban robotic weapons through international treaty. Although automation can lead to greater precision, the United States currently has a directive that humans must be a part of any decision in war involving fatalities. This directive must be kept, but we must also look closely at all of the algorithm-based decisions that lead up to this ultimate point. If they are biased, flawed, or based on incorrect data, then the human will be just as wrong as the machine. The difference, however, between algorithmic bias and the subjectivity of human decision making is that humans trained to kill will sometimes resist doing so on points of conscience. Until we can build ethics, morality, and humanity into machines, the errors of man should be preferable to the precision of machines.

Ultimately, if the state is willing to make digital space a battlefield to be conquered, it remains immensely powerful. But this comes at real costs to the long-term viability of the networked world and to all of its societal benefits. It also represents a predatory view of the social contract underlying the Westphalian order, one that risks the legitimacy of the state itself. The sovereignty—and with it, the power—that citizens willingly give to the state comes with the expectation of protection from physical threats; at the same time, citizens expect the state to govern following the accepted norms of democratic society. Providing security through predatory means, leveraging the comparative advantage the state has over its citizenry, breaks this bargain. And herein lies the crisis facing the state.

CHAPTER NINE

THE CRISIS OF THE STATE

Disruptive innovators empowered by digital technology are chipping away at the institutions that defined international affairs in the 20th century: foreign ministries, armed forces, development agencies, media conglomerates, and international organizations such as the United Nations, the World Bank, and the Red Cross. Some of these institutions are pushing back, at times effectively. But the power dynamic is changing for good, and the implications for the international system are vast. A great rebalancing is under way, and we are only at the beginning. It remains to be seen which traditional institutions will come through this period of turmoil intact, how they will adapt, and to what degree they will remain effective and relevant.

I remain unconvinced that the institutions that served the international community in the 20th century, hierarchical organizations built on an industrial model in an era of command-and-control governance and economic activity, are capable of serving the 21st, which has been defined by decentralization, digital access, and leaps in computational power. For institutions that have struggled to adapt, the problem is not going away. This is less of a radical notion than it once was. In a *Foreign Affairs* article titled

"The Unruled World," governance specialist Patrick Stewart argues that the state-led institutions of the international system are losing their effectiveness, and the future will bring "continued spread of an unattractive but adaptable multilateral sprawl that delivers a partial measure of international cooperation through a welter of informal arrangements and piecemeal approaches." This is what it will look like for states. From the perspective of decentralized and disruptive actors with increasing power, even messy multilateral governance appears both state-centric and of a different era.

Hierarchical institutions are conservative by design. They adapt slowly and cautiously. The international system has evolved with safeguards against rapid evolution for good reason; they are designed to preserve accountability and adhere to the rule of law. Other than moments of crisis, when old norms can be discarded and new ones established, change happens in these institutions through slow learning and rare acts of transformational leadership.[1] There are structural disincentives for reform, too. Having to serve a multitude of interests, large institutions often sacrifice a degree of efficacy in order to preserve legitimacy.[2]

In the private sector, businesses rise, go bankrupt, and disappear, but creative destruction is more difficult in the public sector. Foreign ministries do not simply disappear and get replaced by start-ups. Extinction of state institutions, without replacement with new accountable and effective institutions or networks, will cause real gaps in the international system and leave citizens vulnerable. The status quo has deep flaws, but the costs of state disruption are high; a lack of governance can lead to anarchy, chaos, famine, and war.

The new information environment, however, may require states to adopt some characteristics of start-ups. The challenge for institutions is how to rebuild, reform, reimagine, and disrupt themselves in order to remain relevant in a digital era. For example, the US State Department is experimenting with digital diplomacy, as discussed earlier. The results have been fraught, but it has begun to adapt. At the same time, the state has to determine ways of mitigating the potential harms of networked behavior and use its political, economic, and regulatory powers to incentivize behavior that is broadly in its citizens' interests.

This will be no easy task. As argued throughout this book, the state faces a fundamental crisis. The attributes that empower digital actors (formlessness, instability, and collaborativeness) are the very attributes that traditional state-centric institutions were designed to overcome. While the democratic state serves a wide range of additional functions (providing security, protecting rights and freedoms, delivering social services), and is a highly adaptive institution (the US government of 2014 bears very little resemblance to what it was in 1914), the state's monopoly as a mechanism for collective democratic actions is over. States will therefore have to choose between seeking absolute control and potentially threatening the free and open digital system as well as the principles of democratic governance, or accept a higher degree of uncertainty and give up some power in order to preserve and be a constructive participant in the emergent international system.

———

This crisis of the state has at least four key components: democratic legitimacy, reversing the surveillance state, algorithmic accountability, and Internet governance. Solving the problems posed by any one of them will not prove a panacea for this crisis, nor is this list exhaustive; there are many more innovations being developed and important questions being addressed. But luckily, in each there are individuals and groups experimenting on new models and proposing potential solutions. This is the new landscape in which the state must constructively engage.

DEMOCRATIC LEGITIMACY

The German Pirate Party was founded in 2006 to represent the digital revolution and the transition to the information society. Its positions are closely connected to the global digital activist movement. The party supports government transparency, Internet privacy, civil rights, the free software movement, patent and copyright reform, and net neutrality. After some early success in Germany, the party has spread through Europe, gaining traction in Sweden, Italy, Austria, Norway, France, and the Netherlands. Amelia Andersdotter, a Swedish member of the European Union (EU) Parliament and a digital rights activist, led a common EU Pirate Party platform in the 2014 EU elections.

The Pirate Party also relies on digital technology to re-think the governance processes of traditional political par-ties. Its principal resulting innovation is what it calls liquid democracy. Using an open-source platform labeled Liquid Feedback, all members of the Pirate Party can propose poli-cies. Proposals that receive 10% support from the mem-bership then enter a revision period where alternatives can be proposed, with competing ideas subject to voting. In a process called Global Delegation, members can make other members their proxies, on one issue or for all issues. Del-egates can use the votes they have accrued or hand off their blocks of votes to another party member. (Certain mem-bers have emerged as Pirate Party leaders based on their reputations within the community.) Delegated votes can be reclaimed by members at any time, adding real-time ac-countability to the power these members acquire. As Berlin Pirate Party spokesman Ingo Bormuth told a reporter for *Tech President*, "We want effective people to be powerful and do their work, but we want [the grassroots] to be able to control them."[3]

Fluidity separates delegated democracy from traditional representational democracy, where a single elected official represents his jurisdiction on all topics for a set term. In the Pirate Party system, an expert in a specific topic, say health care, could lead the way on an issue of her exper-tise but stay in the background on other issues. Through Global Delegation, generalists can also emerge as consen-sus leaders.[4]

The Pirate Party sees liquid democracy as an experiment. As Simon Weiss, a Pirate Party politician in the Berlin

Parliament explained, "If you want to propose that as a way of organizing things, you need to see if it actually works, and we're experimenting on ourselves."[5]

While we don't yet know whether liquid democracy works for the Pirate Party, let alone for other parties, the party systems through much of the Western world have atrophied, and the current state of political discourse is grossly out of touch with the technological tools that can enable new systems of policy development and accountability. As we have seen, the state's predatory approach to governance is at odds with the social contact underlying democratic societies, and it risks undermining the very legitimacy with which states have held power. Perhaps even more problematic, the status quo governance discourse delegitimizes many of the emerging actors with real power, and because of this it is blind to some of the core policy challenges of the 21st century. The more experimentation there is on these fronts the better.

And these governance experiments are not limited to new political parties. From Tahrir Square and the wider Arab Spring movement to Occupy Wall Street and its offshoots, a new form of protest movement is afoot. Its organizational tactics and structures arguably point to new forms of ad hoc social organizations to protest perceived abuses of power. They rely on technology to facilitate open communication, avoid hierarchy in their organization and planning, and embrace direct political action against an old world, perceived (rightly or wrongly) as ineffective, corrupt, and statist. As Ricken Patel, president and executive director of Avaaz, a civic organization with over 32 million global members, said of both movements, we are seeing "not just a new media, but a new politics, a new activism. A new democracy. The individual now has unprecedented power to access and publish, to connect, to organize, to affect. Power and agency is spreading out, flattened."[6]

Perhaps most important, as journalist and political scientist Ahmed Teleb points out, in both movements, despite a common opposition toward existing political systems, those involved in each case refused to enter the existing political process in any shape or form, instead hoping to affect the political discourse and the nature of governance from outside the electoral system.[7] This doesn't mean that politicians didn't coopt the activists' rhetoric to garner support. However, Teleb believes that these movements modeled democratic behavior to understand what it means to live in a participatory democracy: "They wanted to see what they were never taught in civics class. What does it mean to deliberate? What does it 'feel' like? In short, they wanted to 'do it themselves.' But technology extended the 'utopianism' past the communal feeling during the encampments and even beyond each movement itself."

These citizen-led experiments with new forms of social organization, governance, and global activism, many of which are at their core technologically enabled, are a sign that new models are both needed and being pushed by those who ultimately feel disenfranchised from our traditional institutions and states.

REVERSING THE SURVEILLANCE STATE

As a consequence of Edward Snowden's revelations we now know how Western democratic states have chosen to respond to the perceived threat of digitally empowered actors. They have sought to control them by, in the words of the NSA, "collecting it all."[8] They have treated the digital network as if it were a new battlefield, one that can be conquered. As has been discussed, the problem with this approach is that in seeking to target perceived threatening disruptive actors, the state risks also shutting down all the positive benefits that the Internet and digital networks allow. In the digital world, the Assad-supported Syrian Electronic Army uses the same tools and tactics as the US-supported Free Syrian Army. What is particularly ironic is that they are heading down this perilous path with the tacit and at times explicit support of the same corporations that have long touted the benefits of disruptive innovation—namely, Silicon Valley.

One underreported aspect of Edward Snowden's NSA revelations has been the close relationship between the US government and technology companies. It was always widely known that the US telecoms functioned as partners in the US surveillance; the legal and logistical infrastructure for wiretapping is built into the regulatory agreements that allow telecoms to operate. But Silicon Valley said it was opposed to clandestine government partnerships, and its prevailing libertarian ethos holds that there is no government service or industry that a technocratic innovation can't efficiently replace. What Evgeny Morozov calls "solutionism" is rooted in a belief that algorithms can replace government.

But as technology companies matured, they increasingly fell under federal regulation. Through e-commerce, Federal Communications Commission (FCC) decisions, free speech legislation, media regulation, patent law, monopoly rulings, international trade law, corporate tax policy, or counterterrorism measures, the state and Silicon Valley have become intertwined, and the big tech companies began courting government and lobbying rather than resisting regulation. Also, Silicon Valley's primary business model depends on large-scale data mining. From Facebook to Google to Yahoo to Twitter, targeted user data became the core monetizable asset of their ostensibly free products. Users entered into a bargain with these companies, trading their personal information (location, friends, photos, personal thoughts, and so on) for the symbiotic benefits of free services and access to the information about others.

This emerging information bargain and the infrastructure built to commercialize it pushed companies closer to the interests of the state. The data storage and analysis capacity they were building was aligned with the surveillance needs of the state. With the passage of the Patriot Act, the United States gained the legal authority to vastly increase its domestic surveillance. But collecting huge amounts of data is hard. It is made immeasurably easier when large, sophisticated companies can do it for you. So, through direct partnerships as well as subversive hacking, the state turned to Silicon Valley to enable its surveillance objectives.

Why did once staunchly libertarian Silicon Valley executives go along with this? First, as explained, they were increasingly dependent on state policy and regulation. They were no longer the scrappy outsiders of corporate America. Second, and I believe more critically, revealing their relationship with the state threatened their core business: collecting data offered to them by their users willingly (and some would argue, naively) for free. In this regard, the NSA revelations threatened Silicon Valley's business model.

While the Pirate Party, Anonymous, and others focus on rights, freedoms, and security, the artificial intelligence pioneer Jaron Lanier has proposed that our data should not be given away for free, a challenge to both the surveillance state and Silicon Valley. In Lanier's view, most citizens' understanding of the relationship between computers and human beings has not kept pace with technology; this lack of knowledge has allowed those who control technology, whether states or large corporations, to have increasing power over society, built on the information we provide freely. Lanier defines information as "a broad term for any conscious intellectual, artistic, or pragmatic contribution to the production of goods, services and cultural output, but it also includes the data that we unconsciously radiate simply by exhibiting certain behavioral and consumer traits."

In the 21st century, information holds the same status that private property did in the early stages of capitalism. Information is private property belonging to individuals, but since its value isn't recognized, corporate giants such as Google and Facebook use it without our consent (and possibly without our knowledge), and we are giving up this economic power without a fight. Therefore, he argues, people need to commodify their data to incentivize the creation of an egalitarian society based on the ethics and principles of free-market capitalism. Lanier's suggestion is that individuals recognize this phenomenon and act as owners of their information.

While Lanier is primarily interested in the digital rights of citizens, his unconventional argument has broad consequence for Western nations that are moving toward becoming surveillance states. If information has economic value, then it is property that cannot be seized by the state.

Ultimately, the surveillance state doesn't just represent the overreaction of the state but is the result of a system of economic and political power under threat. Lanier's argument shows how a very different approach to a problem—in this case, state surveillance and personal privacy and freedom—can lead to entirely new reforms and policies. Whether his suggestion is viable or even the right approach, it is clear to me that if we are going to address the immense challenges outlined throughout this book, we are going to need to step outside the constraints of the traditional policy discourse.

ALGORITHMIC ACCOUNTABILITY

Algorithms have an increasing amount of power over our lives. Whether in policing, border security, drone targeting, tax enforcement, e-commerce, banking, dating, or using social media, it is algorithms that are making decisions for us, often with serious consequences. A white paper from the Institute of the Future predicts that "governance will become automatic, and lawbreaking much more difficult. . . .

Embedded governance will prevent many of the crimes and violations we see today from happening. Firearms will work only when operated by their rightful, registered owners. Office computers will shut down after 40 hours of work unless overtime has been authorized. Disasters and quarantines could also be managed more effectively if information about citizens were known and if laws were downloaded to change behaviors immediately."[9] In this, in my view dystopian, vision moral codes, social norms, and human judgment are augmented or replaced by hidden algorithms and massive data sets, placing a tremendous amount of power in their construction and in the people and institutions that oversee them.

Algorithms are not neutral. They are designed by people, with ideologies, biases, and institutional mandates. Algorithms discriminate and make mistakes. Yet, as computational journalist and computer scientist Nick Diakopoulos argues, the problem with holding algorithms to account is that they are black boxes. We cannot see the Google search algorithm since it is proprietary corporate information, or the algorithm that processes NSA metadata to select drone targets as it is shielded by a national security classification.[10]

But as journalist Andrew Leonard warns, we are increasingly governed by such automated software. "Call it 'algorithmic regulation' or 'embedded governance' or 'automated law enforcement,'" he says, "these built-in systems are sure to become ubiquitous. . . . They will doubtless be quicker to act, more all-seeing and less forgiving than the human-populated bureaucracies that preceded them."[11]

The relationship between algorithms and human interaction has become very important, and to a large extent
invisible. This of course poses a real challenge to governance. How do we regulate something we don't know? One
approach is to start by making these algorithms accountable. A beginning could be to think of them not as un-
knowable black boxes, but as entities that are designed,
built, and have consequence on those who interact with
them. This approach invokes a legal accountability—if
I am harmed by an algorithm, it should be my right to
know how it was built, and how it makes decisions. But
this position also implies a democratic accountability. As
a democratic society, we have in the past agreed to collective rules of behavior and norms of governance. But this
required mechanisms through which we can know how
we are governed. If algorithms represent a new ungoverned
space, a new public, then they are an affront to our very
system of governance, one that requires a degree of transparency and accountability in order to function. A public
space that exists outside of these bounds is a threat to the
notion of collective governance itself. This at its core, is a
profoundly libertarian notion—one that states will have to
engage with seriously if they are going to remain relevant
to their digital citizenry.[12]

INTERNET GOVERNANCE

One of the compelling aspects of the Internet is the empowerment that can emerge from universal access to a common
technology. While political, economic, and social factors

influence access to the Internet, once a user is online he or she can do the same thing anywhere in the world. It is this common freedom to explore, learn, communicate, and build that has generated many of the benefits of the Internet. And this universality explains why the Internet rights movement puts so much emphasis on access, privacy, and online security, and resists state censorship and corporate control so strongly.

There have always been those who wanted to control the Internet. Autocratic regimes seek to monitor, censor, restrict, and control access in their countries. As we have seen in the Arab Spring uprisings, the very technology that can allow people to organize, find common cause, and push back against hierarchical power can also be a remarkable tool of surveillance and social control. In 2015, the international community will renegotiate the UN treaty concerning the governance of the Internet. On one side of the negotiations, the United States and its allies want to keep the Internet run by a small group of nonprofit organizations based in the United States. On the other side are states including Russia, China, Brazil, India, and Iran, who want a new global body to oversee the Internet.

In China, Russia, and Iran, we are seeing a renewed push toward either mass censorship and control or, more drastically, the creation of national Internets cut off from the rest of the world. Balkanization of the Internet received a boost from the actions of the NSA revealed by Edward Snowden. In April 2014, Vladimir Putin, president of Russia, told a media conference in St. Petersburg that the Internet was built by the CIA as tool for global espionage and hinted that he wants to build a Russian-run alternative. China was supposed to be a major market for Internet-based growth, but in light of the NSA actions, it has made US firms like IBM and Oracle targets of the Chinese Ministry of Public Security, making it far more difficult for them to do business there.

This concept of multiple Internets, also referred to as the "splinternet," is not only coming from autocrats. In light of NSA revelations, the EU and BRICS (Brazil, Russia, India, China, and South Africa) are shifting away from US-based technologies, companies, and servers toward national and regional Internet infrastructure. A report from the London School of Economics (LSE) Media Policy Project outlines how these countries are becoming increasingly concerned about "privacy sovereignty" and want greater technical control over the Internet. Brazil and Germany are pushing to pass national laws "requiring data pertaining to their citizens to be stored locally instead of shipped around the Internet into the purview of the NSA," the report says. And EU countries are considering revoking data-sharing agreements with the United States. (It is debatable whether this would actually protect them against NSA spying, as many of these "local" companies are actually subsidiaries of US corporations and therefore still subject to US law.)[13]

In a speech at the General Assembly of the United Nations, Brazilian President Dilma Rouseff called on others to disconnect from the US Internet and develop their own technical and governance structures. Brazil is trying to "lay cables" across South America and beyond, including a 34,000 km undersea fiber-optic cable from Vladivostok to

Fortaleza (via Shantou, Chennai, and Cape Town), making it a completely BRICS network. Sascha Meinrath, founder of the Open Technology Institute, writes, "The Internet is in danger of becoming like the European train system, where varying voltage and 20 different types of signaling technologies force operators to stop and switch systems or even to another locomotive, resulting in delays, inefficiencies, and higher costs."[14]

While states are seeking to create national Internets, individuals and groups are making their own micro networks, either to provide access to users outside of large telecom and Internet service provider (ISP) networks or to operate beyond state and corporate control. Local mesh networks can connect to the wider Internet via any of their nodes or exist completely off the grid. Project Meshnet was created by a group of Reddit users seeking to "create a versatile, decentralized network built on secure protocols for routing traffic over private mesh or public Internet works independent of a central supporting infrastructure."[15] They explain that the Internet Corporation for Assigned Names and Numbers (ICANN)—and, by extension, the US government—controls the basic structure of the Internet, and they advocate radical decentralization of the Internet architecture through local mesh networks that allow for end-to-end encrypted traffic "completely immune" to any form of censorship. These networks "can be stitched together from many types of physical links— WiFi, fiber optic, free space optical, Ethernet cables—into one consistently-accessible microcosm of the greater global network."[16]

Mesh networks are catching on internationally as well. The *New Scientist* reported on a meshwork in Catalonia, Spain, called Guifi that in August 2013 had more than 21,000 nodes. Guifi can host web servers, video conferencing, and radio broadcasts, and would remain online even if the rest of Spain were to experience an Internet blackout.[17] A similar project in Greece called the Athens Wireless Metropolitan Network comprises more than 1,000 rooftop antennas. As one of its users stated, "when you run your own network, nobody can shut it down."[18]

Likewise, even as UN negotiations seek to regulate the Internet's domain name system (DNS), new parallel systems are being developed. One called the Open and Decentralized DNS (ODDNS) is based on a peer-to-peer network that openly shares both the domain names and related Internet Protocol (IP) addresses of its users. Its creator, Jimmy Rudolf, says he built the system to "show governments that it is not possible to prevent people from talking."[19] As one hacker told essayist Michael Gross, "The more government tries to regulate, the more people will try to build an Internet that is uncensorable and unfilterable and unblockable." They will circumvent state control.

Even worse, as Yochai Benkler states, fighting against this tide will put governments "at odds with some of the most energetic and wired segments of society." This has real policy consequences: "Any society that commits itself to eliminating what makes Anonymous possible and powerful risks losing the openness and uncertainty that have made the Internet home to so much innovation, expression, and creativity."[20]

The obvious question to emerge from both the splinternet and meshnet trends is where they leave the US government, the Internet Corporation for Assigned Names and Numbers (ICANN), and the range of Internet governance organizations that are increasingly marginalized in their oversight of what is more and more seen as a global commons. If a government cares about protecting and empowering individuals, then protecting their freedom online should be a focal point of foreign policy. Yet the states renegotiating the UN Internet treaty oppose having someone at the negotiating table who represents those individuals and groups who make up the online network.

What would a state's policy toward the Internet look like if it were to embrace the voices, values, and attributes of those who live in the networked world? What if a foreign policy were to assertively seek to protect the very foundation of the system that powers the 21st century?

———

In a thoughtful essay titled "Code as Power: How the New World Order Is Reinforcing the Old," Jordan McCarthy of the Open Technology Institute cites Internet rights pioneer John Perry Barlow's Declaration of the Independence of Cyberspace. Barlow is optimistic about the power of decentralized networks to push back against the more oppressive systems of economic and political governance. For Barlow, the digital realm "is an act of nature . . . [growing] itself through our collective actions." It is a place, he says, where "legal concepts of property, expression, identity, movement, and context do not apply;" where "anyone . . . may express his or her beliefs, no matter how singular, without fear of being coerced into silence or conformity"; where "governance will emerge . . . from ethics, enlightened self-interest, and the commonweal."[21]

But as we have seen, while digital technology has enabled decentralized actors, digital technologies in and of themselves are not neutral tools. They empower those who build and understand how to use them. The demise of traditional institutions is therefore not the only option of the digital revolution; rather, there is a possibility that these institutions will restructure themselves around the capabilities of new technologies. In many cases, those that are best positioned to benefit from the power of code are existing institutions. And in contrast to disruption theory, this is what many institutions have done: coopted technologies and aligned them with their core objectives. If traditional and powerful institutions can shape the nature of technologies like Bitcoin then it will surely limit their disruptive potential. But the crypto-anarchists are not going away, and there is very little the state can do to stop them.

There are some things the states and their foreign policies could do to signal willingness to engage in the digital conversation.

First, states could embrace disruption. Rather than moving state-based institutions of a bygone era online, states must promote a reengineering of the international system. To do this requires identifying those actors that make the best use of the contemporary network and scaling them so as to engender a new type of international institution. States must grasp the full range of disruption that groups like Anonymous represent in order to determine new ways to model institutional design and behavior. Our current global institutions were designed by, built for, and are run by the actors who had power in the 20th century. But what would an international organization look like that included the actors we now know have power in the digital world? What would it mean to include elements of Anonymous and Telecomix in an international organization? For one, it would take radically different notions of what an institution is and how it functions.

Second, a truly networked foreign policy would seek to protect the network at all costs. To complement these new actors in the promotion of individual rights and freedoms, states must fundamentally rethink online governance. Rather than seeing online governance as a way of regulating these private actors, states must accept that these new actors are not only self-regulating (and perhaps beyond regulation) but also are key to the delivery of individual rights and freedoms. They can be allies in implementing the collective action of the democratic state. It is thus in the state's interest to protect the system that allows these new private actors to flourish.

Third, states should support empowering technologies. The contemporary international network, complex as it is, positions states in multiple roles: as producers, consumers, and mediators of technology. At the center of this role lies a paradox: the tools that enable autocratic governments to monitor and control their citizens are produced by Western technology companies. States seeking an international agenda that foregrounds the individual must recognize these contradictions and ensure that they consistently act in the name of individual rights and freedoms.

There remains an alternate temptation, however, which I worry will prove determinative. As the earlier exploration of the algorithmic violence suggested, the state is able to marshal digital technology, often to significant effect. The ethical costs are very high, but the state has an option to seek absolute control of the digital ecosystem. But in seeking to limit the perceived threats of digital empowerment, they will ultimately destroy the benefits. Ultimately, states will have to choose between giving up some power and control in order to preserve the emerging system, or seek absolute control.

The Treaty of Westphalia, signed in 1648, ended a century-long period of conflict and instability between warring disparate empires. These empires, once the absolute ruling powers, were losing control, over both their territory and their citizens, in part because of the introduction of a wide range of new technologies. By legitimizing the state as the primary sovereign unit of the international system, and giving it power and responsibility over the well-being of its citizens, the treaty created order and stability out of what was an increasingly chaotic global system.

We face a similar moment today. States as the primary unit of the international system are being challenged for both power and legitimacy by a wide range of new individuals, groups, and ad hoc networks, all empowered by digital technology. While the state has the power to fight back, it does so at the risk of jeopardizing the emerging system.

What is yet to be seen is whether a similar restructuring of power can take place in a digitally enabled world, without its empowering chaos, messiness, and disorder being lost.

NOTES

CHAPTER I

1. Kelly, Brian. (2012). "Investing in a Centralized Cybersecurity Infrastructure: Why 'Hacktivism' Can and Should Influence Cybersecurity Reform," *Boston University Law Review* 92.5: 1663–1710, p. 1678.
2. Landers, Chris. (2008). "Serious Business: Anonymous Takes on Scientology," *CityPaper*, April 2, www2.citypaper.com/columns/story.asp?id=15,543.
3. Benkler, Yochai. (2012). "Hacks of Valor: Why Anonymous Is Not a Threat to National Security," *Foreign Affairs*, April 4, www.foreignaffairs.com/articles/137382/yochai-benkler/hacks-of-valor.
4. "Anonymous gain access to FBI and Scotland Yard hacking call," *BBC*, February 3, 2012, http://www.bbc.com/news/world-us-canada-16875921.
5. "FBI names, arrests Anon who infiltrated its secret conference call," *Art Technica*, March 6, 2012, http://arstechnica.com/tech-policy/2012/03/fbi-names-arrests-anon-who-infiltrated-its-secret-conference-call/.
6. "'Anonymous' Follows Hacking Of FBI-Scotland Yard Phone Call With Attacks," *NPR*, February 3, 2012, http://www.npr.org/blogs/thetwo-way/2012/02/03/146350626/anonymous-follows-hacking-of-fbi-scotland-yard-phone-call-with-attacks.

7. As cited in Sengupta, Somini. (2012). "The Soul of the New Hacktivist," *New York Times*, March 17, www.nytimes.com/2012/03/18/sunday-review/the-soul-of-the-new-hacktivist.html?_r=0.

8. Bower, Joseph L., and Clayton M. Christensen. (1995). "Disruptive Technologies: Catching the Wave," *Harvard Business Review*, January, http://hbr.org/1995/01/disruptive-technologies-catching-the-wave/.

9. Clayton, Christensen. (2011). *The Innovator's Dilemma: The Revolutionary Book That Will Change the Way You Do Business.* New York: Harper Business (first published in 1997).

10. Christensen, Clayton, Heiner Baumann, Rudy Ruggles, and Thomas M. Sadtler. (2006). "Disruptive Innovation for Social Change," *Harvard Business Review*, December, http://hbr.org/2006/12/disruptive-innovation-for-social-change/ar/1.

11. "Planet Blue Coat: Mapping Global Censorship and Surveillance Tools," *Citizen Lab*, January 2013, https://citizenlab.org/wp-content/uploads/2012/07/01-2011-behindbluecoat.pdf.

12. "Pentagon Bans Towleroad, AMERICAblog Sites for Being 'LGBT.' Coulter, Limbaugh OK," http://americablog.com/2013/01/pentagon-bans-gay-web-sites.html.

13. Gallagher, Ryan. (2011). "Governments Turn to Hacking Techniques for Surveillance of Citizens," *Guardian*, November 1, www.theguardian.com/technology/2011/nov/01/governments-hacking-techniques-surveillance.

14. Marks, Paul. (2011). "Global Surveillance Supermarket Offered to Dictators." *One Per Cent*, December 1, www.newscientist.com/blogs/onepercent/2011/12/surveillance-supermarket-offer.html.

15. Morozov, Evgeny. (2011). "Political Repression 2.0," *New York Times*, September 1, www.nytimes.com/2011/09/02/opinion/political-repression-2-0.html?_r=0.

16. Horwitz, Sari, Shyamantha Asokan, and Julie Tate. (2011). "Trade in Surveillance Technology Raises Worries," *Washington Post*, December 1, www.washingtonpost.com/world/national-security/trade-in-surveillance-technology-raises-worries/2011/11/22/gIQAFFZOGO_story.html.

17. "Enemies of the Internet: Surveillance Dealerships," Reporters without Borders, March 2014, http://12mars.rsf.org/2014-en/2014/03/11/arms-trade-fairs-surveillance-dealerships/.

18. Gallagher, "Governments Turn to Hacking Techniques."

19. Newton-Small, Jay. (2012). "Hillary's Little Startup: How the U.S. Is Using Technology to Aid Syria's Rebels," *TIME*, June 13, http://world.time.com/2012/06/13/hillarys-little-startup-how-the-u-s-is-using-technology-to-aid-syrias-rebels/#ixzz2dxRqAD6q.

20. Peterson, Andrea. (2013). "The U.S. Isn't Bombing Syria Yet. But It Is Providing Tech Support to the Rebels," *Washington Post*, September 3, www.washingtonpost.com/blogs/the-switch/wp/2013/09/03/the-u-s-isnt-bombing-syria-yet-but-it-is-providing-tech-support-to-the-rebels/.

21. Crawford, Jamie. (2012). "U.S. Aid to Syrian Opposition Includes Specialized Communications Equipment," *CNN*, April 2, http://security.blogs.cnn.com/2012/04/02/u-s-aid-to-syrian-opposition-includes-specialized-communications-equipment/.

22. Newton-Small, "Hillary's Little Startup."

23. 9/11 is the date of three related terrorist attacks in the United States.

24. Kopstein, Joshua. (2014). "The NSA Can 'Collect-It-All,' but What Will It Do with Our Data Next?" *Daily Beast*, May 16, www.thedailybeast.com/articles/2014/05/16/the-nsa-can-collect-it-all-but-what-will-it-do-with-our-data-next.html.

25. Kopstein, "The NSA Can "Collect-It-All."

26. Norton, Quinn. (2014). "A Day of Speaking Truth to Power: Visiting the ODNI," *Medium*, March 12, https://medium.com/quinn-norton/dbc0669aa9ca.

27. "How Al-Qaeda Uses Encryption Post-Snowden (Part 2)—New Analysis in Collaboration with ReversingLabs," *Recorded Future*, August 1, 2014, www.recordedfuture.com/al-qaeda-encryption-technology-part-2/.

CHAPTER 2

1. Lamborn, Alan C., and Joseph Lepgold. (2002). *World Politics into the 21st Century: Unique Contexts, Enduring Patterns*. Upper Saddle River, NJ: Prentice Hall.

2. Clark, William R., Matt Golder, and Sona N. Golder. (2012). "The Origins of the Modern State," in *Principles of Comparative Politics*. London: Sage, https://files.nyu.edu/sln202/public/chapter4.pdf.

3. Hobbes, Thomas. (1994). *Leviathan*. Edwin Curley, ed. Indianapolis, IN: Hackett, pp. 75–76.

4. Carneiro, Robert L. (1970). "A Theory of the Origin of the State," *Science* 169.3947: 733–738, http://abuss.narod.ru/Biblio/carneiro_origin.htm.

5. Tilly, Charles. (1985). "War Making and State Making as Organized Crime," in *Bringing Back the State*, ed. Peter Evans, Dietrich Rueschemeyer, and Theda Skocpol. Cambridge: Cambridge University Press.

6. North, Douglass. (1981). *Structure and Change in Economic History*. New York: W.W. Norton.

7. Ahmad, Rana E., and Abida Eijaz. (2011). "Modern Sovereign State System Is under Cloud in the Age of Globalization," *South Asian Studies* 26.2: 285–297.

8. Held, David, and Anthony McGrew. (1998). "The End of the Old Order? Globalization and the Prospects for World Order," *Review of International Studies* 24.5: 219–245.

9. Keohane, Robert O., and Joseph S. Nye Jr. (1998). "Power and Interdependence in the Information Age," *Foreign Affairs* 77.5: 81–94.

10. Castells, Manuel. (2004). "Afterword: Why Networks Matter," *Demos*, online archive, http://www.demos. co.uk/files/File/networklogic17castells.pdf.

11. Castells, "Afterword."

12. Castells, "Afterword."

13. Kahler, Miles, ed. (2009). *Networked Politics: Agency, Power, and Governance*. Ithaca, NY: Cornell University Press.

14. Kahler, *Networked Politics*.

15. Lake, David A., and Wendy Wong. (2009). "The Politics of Networks: Interests, Power, and Human Rights Norms," in *Networked Politics: Agency, Power, and Governance*, ed. Miles Kahler. Ithaca, NY: Cornell University Press, pp. 27–150.

16. Shirky, Clay. (2008). *Here Comes Everybody: The Power of Organizing without Organizations*. New York: Penguin Press.

17. Benkler, Yochai. (2011). "Networks of Power, Degrees of Freedom," *International Journal of Communication* 5: 721–755.

18. Benkler, "Networks of Power."

19. Slaughter, Anne Marie. (2009). "America's Edge: Power in the Networked Century," *Foreign Affairs* 88.1: 94–113.

20. Kahler, *Networked Politics.*

21. Slaughter, Anne Marie. (2004). "Sovereignty and Power in a Networked World Order," *Stanford Journal of International Law* 40: 283.

22. Slaughter, "America's Edge."

23. Slaughter, "Sovereignty and Power," p. 283.

24. Ammori, Marvin. (2005). "Private Regulation, Free Speech, and Lessons from the Sinclair Blogstorm," *Michigan Telecommunications and Technology Law Review* 12.1: 1–75, pp. 43–46.

25. Froomkin, Michael. (1997). "The Internet as a Source of Regulatory Arbitrage," in *Borders in Cyberspace: Information Policy and the Global Information Infrastructure*, ed. Brian Kahin and Charles Nesson. Cambridge, MA: MIT Press, p. 129.

26. Albert, Reka, Hawoong Jeong, and Albert-László Barabási. (2000). "Error and Attack Tolerance of Complex Networks," *Nature* 406: 378–382.

27. Froomkin, "The Internet."

28. Godin, Seth. (2001). *Unleashing the Ideasvirus.* Dobbs Ferry, NY: Hyperion.

29. Morozov, Evgeny. (2011). *The Net Delusion: The Dark Side of Internet Freedom.* New York: Public Affairs.

30. Ammori, "Private Regulation."

31. Lessig, Lawrence. (1998). "The New Chicago School," *Journal of Legal Studies* 27.S2: 661–691.

32. Benkler, Yochai. *The Wealth of Networks: How Social Production Transforms Markets and Freedom.* New Haven, CT: Yale University Press, http://cyber.law.harvard.edu/wealth_of_networks/index.php?title=Text_Part_One.

33. Sundén, Jenny. (2003). *Material Virtualities: Approaching Online Textual Embodiment*. New York: Peter Lang.

34. Castells, Manuel. (2000). "Information Technology and Global Capitalism," in *On the Edge: Living with Global Capitalism*, ed. Will Hutton and Anthony Giddens. London: Jonathan Cape.

35. Wendt, Alexander. (1992). "Anarchy Is What States Make of It," *International Organization* 46.2: 392.

36. boyd, danah. (2008). "Why Youth (Heart) Social Network Sites: The Role of Networked Publics in Teenage Social Life," in *Youth, Identity and Digital Media*, ed. D. Buckingham. Cambridge, MA: MIT Press, pp. 119–142.

37. Haythornthwaite, Caroline. (2005). "Social Networks and Internet Connectivity Effects," *Information, Communication & Society* 8.2: 125–147.

38. Shirky, Clay. (2001). "Listening to Napster," in *Peer-to-Peer: Harnessing the Power of Disruptive Technologies*, ed. Andy Oram. Sebastopol: O'Reilly and Associates.

39. Shirky, *Here Comes Everybody*.

40. Considine, Mark. (2005). "Partnerships and Collaborative Advantage: Some Reflections on New Forms of Network Governance," background paper, Centre for Public Policy, December 14.

41. Castells, "Information Technology and Global Capitalism."

CHAPTER 3

1. Greenberg, Andy. (2011). "Meet Telecomix, the Hackers Bent on Exposing Those Who Censor and Surveil the Internet," *Forbes*, December 26, www.forbes.com/sites/

andygreenberg/2011/12/26/meet-telecomix-the-hackers-bent-on-exposing-those-who-censor-and-surveil-the-in-ternet/.

2. Fein, Peter. (2011). "Hacking for Freedom," http://i. wearpants.org/blog/hacking-for-freedom/.

3. KheOps.(2011). "#OpSyria:When the Internet Does Not Let Citizens Down," *Reflets.info*, September 11, http://reflets.info/opsyria-when-the-internet-does-not-let-citizens-down/.

4. KheOps, "#OpSyria."

5. Greenberg, "Meet Telecomix."

6. Fein, Peter. (2012). "Democracy Is Obsolete," paper pre-sented at the Personal Democracy Forum conference, www.youtube.com/watch?v=SsW4rASigao.

7. Fitri, Nofia. (2011). "Democracy Discourses through the Internet Communication: Understanding the Hacktiv-ism for the Global Changing," *Online Journal of Com-munication and Media Technologies* 1.2 (April), www. ojcmt.net/articles/12/121.pdf.

8. Arendt, Hannah. (2012). *In der Gegenwart: Übungen im politischen Denken II.* München: Piper. In English: Arendt, H. (1972). *Crises of the Republic: Lying in Politics, Civil Disobedience on Violence, Thoughts on Politics, and Revolution* (Vol. 219). Boston: Hough-ton Mifflin Harcourt, p. 299. Cited in "Re-thinking Civil Disobedience," by Theresa Züger, in *Internet Policy Review*, http://policyreview.info/articles/analysis/re-thinking-civil-disobedience.

9. Philosopher and constitutional theorist Ronald Dworkin identifies three forms of civil disobedience. "Integrity-based" civil disobedience occurs when a citizen dis-obeys a law she or he feels is immoral, as in the case of

Northerners disobeying the fugitive slave laws by refusing to turn over escaped slaves to authorities. "Justice-based" civil disobedience occurs when a citizen disobeys laws in order to lay claim to some right denied to her or him, as when blacks illegally protested during the civil rights movement. "Policy-based" civil disobedience occurs when a person breaks the law in order to change a policy he or she believes is dangerously wrong. It is these rationales, and the related degrees to which the law should be obeyed in society, which form the core of most debates over the bounds of civil disobedience. To Howard Zinn, "There is no social value to a general obedience to the law, any more than there is value to a general disobedience to the law." That is, "It becomes not only justifiable but necessary when a fundamental human right is at stake, and when legal channels are inadequate for securing that right." In 1961, philosophy scholar Hugo Adam Bedau defined civil disobedience as "a public, non-violent political act contrary to law and carried out with the aim of bringing about change in law or policy." This articulation was later broadened by Badau to include acts which fall within the bounds of the law. Also capturing this sense of protest, political philosophy scholar Robin Celikates defines civil disobedience as an "intentionally unlawful collective protest action, which is based on principles and aims at changing (as in preventing or enforcing) certain laws or political steps." Joseph Raz, who argues that there is no obligation to obey the law, even in a society whose legal system is just, echoes this.

10. McCormick, Ty. (2013). "A Short History of Hacktivism," *Canberra Times*, May 10, www.canberratimes.

com.au/technology/technology-news/a-short-history-of-hacktivism-20,130,510-2jbv0.html.

11. Norton, Quinn. (2013). "The Words of a Troll," *Medium*, https://medium.com/quinn-norton/the-words-of-a-troll-d3ed1ce63615.

12. Ludlow, Peter. (2010). "WikiLeaks and Hacktivist Culture," *The Nation*, September 15, www.thenation.com/article/154780/wikileaks-and-hacktivist-culture%22%20%5Cl%20%22ixzz2VY3w0FXN.

13. Critical Art Ensemble. (1996). "Electronic Civil Disobedience and Other Unpopular Ideas," www.critical-art.net/books/ecd/.

14. Sauter, Molly. (2013). "The Future of Civil Disobedience Online," *io9*, June 17, http://io9.com/the-future-of-civil-disobedience-online-512,193,648.

15. Sauter, "The Future of Civil Disobedience Online."

16. In her political science PhD thesis on hacktivism, Alexandra Samuel builds a typology of hacktivism that shows how damaging it is to militarize or securitize the language and policy around a very broad set of actions and actors. Samuels defines activism as "the nonviolent use of illegal or legally ambiguous digital tools in pursuit of political ends," but then places this definition within a broad range of activities that each sit on a spectrum of illegality and potential malicious intent. This includes civil disobedience as both physical and online virtual sit-ins; online activism, including everything from movement building as with MoveOn.org, to formal political campaigning; hacking, which can be explicitly political or apolitical; and cyberterrorism, which ranges from transgressive behavior online to actions intended to

cross over into violence in the physical world, such as hacking an air traffic control tower to crash a plane.

17. Ronfeldt, David, and John Arquilla. (2001). "Networks, Netwar and the Fight for the Future," *First Monday* 6.7 (October), http://ojphi.org/ojs/index.php/fm/article/view/889/798.

18. Ronfeldt and Arquilla, "Networks, Netwar and the Fight for the Future."

19. Denning, D. E. (2000). "Cyberterrorism: Testimony before the Special Oversight Panel on Terrorism, Committee on Armed Services, US House of Representatives" (Vol. 23). Washington, DC, May.

20. Coleman, G. (2013). "Anonymous in Context: The Politics and Power behind the Mask," *Internet Governance Papers*, 3.

21. Statement by Chris Hedges in support of Jeremy Hammond's call for a fair trial, November 29, 2012, http://andystepanian.tumblr.com/post/36815485693/statement-by-chris-hedges-in-support-of-jeremy.

22. Vivien Lesnik Weisman. (2013). "Weev, the Hacker Who Didn't Hack AT&T," *Huffington Post*, March 25, www.huffingtonpost.com/vivien-lesnik-weisman/weev-hacker-att_b_2,948,173.html.

23. Dishneau, David. (2013). "Audio of Bradley Manning explaining why he leaked U.S. secrets posted online. CTV News," March 12, www.ctvnews.ca/world/audio-of-bradley-manning-explaining-why-he-leaked-u-s-secrets-posted-online-1.1192840#ixzz31vWOJXKK.

24. Worthington, Andy. (2013). "UN Torture Rapporteur Accuses US Government of Cruel and Inhuman Treatment of Bradley Manning," *Andy Worthington Blog*,

March 12, www.andyworthington.co.uk/2012/03/13/
un-torture-rapporteur-accuses-us-government-of-cruel-
and-inhuman-treatment-of-bradley-manning/#sthash.
kqmmqfHZ.dpuf.

25. Sullivan, Margaret. (2013). "The Danger of Suppressing
the Leaks," *New York Times*, March 3, www.nytimes.
com/2013/03/10/public-editor/the-danger-of-suppressing-
the- leaks.html?ref=bradleyemanning.

26. Abrams, Floyd, and Yochai Benkler. (2013). "Death
to Whistleblowers?" *New York Times*, March 13,
www.nytimes.com/2013/03/14/opinion/the-impact-of-
the-bradley-manning-case.html?_r=0.

27. Hanna Arendt Center. (2011). "Civil Disobedience and
O.W.S.," November 16, www.hannaharendtcenter.org/?
p=2705.

CHAPTER 4

1. Anderson, Nate, and Cyrus Farviar. (2012). "How the
Feds Took Down the Dread Pirate Roberts," *Arstechnica*,
October 3, http://arstechnica.com/tech-policy/2013/10/
how-the-feds-took-down-the-dread-pirate-roberts/.

2. Greenberg, Andy. (2013). "Follow the Bitcoins: How
We Got Busted Buying Drugs on Silk Road's Black
Market," *Forbes*, September 5, www.forbes.com/sites/
andygreenberg/2013/09/05/follow-the-bitcoins-how-
we-got-busted-buying-drugs-on-silk-roads-black-
market/.

3. Greenberg, "Follow the Bitcoins."

4. Patrick, Brian Eha. (2013). "Could the Silk Road Closure
Be Good for Bitcoin?" *New Yorker*, October 5, www.

newyorker.com/online/blogs/currency/ 2013/10/could-the-silk-road-closure-be-good-for-bitcoin.html.

5. Greenberg, "Follow the Bitcoins."

6. "Silk Road Returns: New Owner Aims to 'Double the Achievements' of the First Site." (2013). *Belfast Telegraph*, November 8, www.belfasttelegraph.co.uk/life/technology-gadgets/silk-road-returns-new-owner-aims-to-double-the-achievements-of-the-first-site-29736863.html.

7. Patrick, "Could the Silk Road Closure Be Good for Bitcoin?"

8. Patrick, "Could the Silk Road Closure Be Good for Bitcoin?"

9. Spaven, Emily. (2013). "Robocoin Bitcoin ATM Takes More Than CA$1m in 29 Days," *CoinDesk*, November 27, www.coindesk.com/robocoin-bitcoin-atm-cad1m-29-days/.

10. Eastwood, Joel. (2013). "Bitcoin Entrepreneurs Want to Put Virtual Coins in Your Wallet," *Toronto Star*, November 12, www.thestar.com/news/gta/2013/11/12/bitcoin_entrepreneurs_want_to_put_virtual_coins_in_your_wallet.html#.

11. Burgoyne, Matthew. (2014). "Does Canada View Bitcoin as Currency?" *CoinDesk*, accessed February 2, 2014, www.coindesk.com/canada-view-bitcoin-currency/.

12. Hassleback, Drew. (2014). "Governments Ponder Legitimacy of Bitcoins," *Financial Post*, accessed February 2, http://business.financialpost.com/2013/11/19/governments-ponder-legitimacy-of-bitcoins/.

13. Luff, Jonathan, and Alec Ross. (2013). "Why Bitcoin Is on the Money," *Telegraph.co.uk*, June 24, www.

telegraph.co.uk/finance/currency/10139651/Why-Bitcoin-is-on-the-money.html.

14. Steil, Benn, and Manuel Hinds. (2009). *Money, Markets, and Sovereignty*. New Haven, CT: Yale University Press.

15. Steil and Hinds, *Money, Markets, and Sovereignty*.

16. Rousseau, P. (2004). "A Common Currency: Early US Monetary Policy and the Transition to the Dollar," *National Bureau of Economic Research*, August, www.nber.org/papers/w10702.pdf?new_window=1.

17. Schwartz, Pedro. (2013). "Why the Euro Failed and How It Will Survive," *Cato Journal* 33.3.

18. Cohen, B. J. (2012). "The Future of the Euro: Let's Get Real." *Review of International Political Economy* 19.4: 689–700.

19. Davis, Joshua. (2011). "The Cryptocurrency," *New Yorker*, October, www.newyorker.com/reporting/2011/10/10/111010fa_fact_davis.

20. Lach, Eric. (2011). "Feds Seeking $7M Worth of Privately-Minted 'Liberty Dollars,'" *Talking Points Memo*, April 4, accessed August 16, 2012, http://talkingpointsmemo.com/muckraker/feds-seeking-7m-worth-of-privately-minted-liberty-dollars.

21. Lovett, Tom. (2011). "Local Liberty Dollar 'Architect' Bernard von NotHaus Convicted," *Evansville Courier & Press*, March 19, www.courierpress.com/news/2011/mar/19/local-liberty-dollar-architect-found-guilty/.

22. US Department of Justice. (2011). "Digital Currency Business E-Gold Indicted for Money Laundering and Illegal Money Transmitting," April 27.

23. Bartlett, Jamie, Carl Miller, James Smith, and Louis Reynolds. (2013). "Heads Up: Bitcoin an Introductory

CASM Briefing." *Demos*, p. 4, www.demos.co.uk/files/ Heads_Up_-_web.pdf?1387559230.

24. Bartlett et al., "Heads Up."

25. Nakamoto, Satoshi. (2008). "Bitcoin: A Peer-to-Peer Electronic Cash System." http://bitcoin.org/bitcoin.pdf.

26. Andreessen, Marc. (2013). "Why Bitcoin Matters," *NYTimes.com*., January 21, accessed February 4, 2014, http://dealbook.nytimes.com/2014/01/21/why-bitcoin-matters/?_php=true&_type=blogs&_r=0.

27. Lee, Timothy B. (2011). "Bitcoin's Collusion Problem," Bottom-Up, April 19, accessed February 4, 2014, http://timothyblee.com/2011/04/19/bitcoins-collusion-problem/.

28. Andreessen, "Why Bitcoin Matters."

29. Bloomberg. (2014). *Kenya*, http://mobile.bloomberg.com/topics/kenya/.

30. Andreessen, "Why Bitcoin Matters."

31. McGuire, Patrick. (2013). "Bitcoin Has Already Morphed Society," *Vice*, November 28, www.vice.com/en_ca/read/bitcoin-has-already-morphed-society.

32. Cowen, Tyler. (2011). "The Economics of Bitcoin," *Marginal Revolution*, April 19, http://marginalrevolution.com/marginalrevolution/2011/04/the-economics-of-bitcoin.html.

33. Payne, Alex. (2013). "Bitcoin, Magical Thinking, and Political Ideology," *Alex Payne* (blog), https://al3x.net/2013/12/18/bitcoin.html.

34. Stross, Charlie. (2013). "Why I Want Bitcoin to Die in a Fire," *Charlie's Diary* (blog), December 8, www.antipope.org/charlie/blog-static/2013/12/why-i-want-bitcoin-to-die-in-a.html.

35. Lee, "Bitcoin's Collusion Problem."

36. Salmon, Felix. (2014). "The Bitcoin Bubble and the Future of Currency—Money & Banking—Medium," accessed February 4, https://medium.com/money-banking/2b5ef79482cb.

37. Carney, Michael. (2013). "Bitcoin Has a Dark Side: Its Carbon Footprint," *PandoDaily*, December 16, http://pando.com/2013/12/16/bitcoin-has-a-dark-side-its-carbon-footprint/.

38. May, Timothy C. (1994). *The Cyphernomicon*, www.cypherpunks.to/faq/cyphernomicron/cyphernomicon.txt.

39. "Crypto-Anarchy and Libertarian Entrepreneurship—Chapter 3: The Killer App of Liberty." (2013). *The Mises Circle* (blog), May 29, http://themisescircle.org/blog/2013/05/29/crypto-anarchy-and-libertarian-entrepreneurship-chapter-iii/.

40. *The Mises Circle.*

41. May, Timothy C. (1992). *The Crypto-Anarchist Manifesto*, http://groups.csail.mit.edu/mac/classes/6.805/articles/crypto/cypherpunks/may-crypto-manifesto.html.

42. Salmon, "The Bitcoin Bubble."

43. Bohm, Paul. (2011). "Bitcoin's Value Is Decentralization," *Paul Bohm's Blog*, June 17, accessed February 5, 2014, http://paulbohm.com/articles/bitcoins-value-is-decentralization/.

44. Salmon, "The Bitcoin Bubble."

45. Salmon, "The Bitcoin Bubble."

46. Buffet, Warren. (2012). "Warren Buffet: Why Stocks Beat Gold and Bonds." *Fortune*, http://fortune.com/2012/02/09/warren-buffett-why-stocks-beat-gold-and-bonds/.

47. *Bitcoin Dark Wallet* (campaign), www.indiegogo.com/
projects/bitcoin-dark-wallet#home.

48. Ramos, Jairo. (2014). "A Native American Tribe
Hopes Digital Currency Boosts Its Sovereignty," *NPR
Code Switch*, March 7, www.npr.org/blogs/codeswit
ch/2014/03/07/287258968/a-native-american-tribe-
hopes-digital-currency-boosts-its-sovereignty.

CHAPTER 5

1. Brenner, Marie. (2012). "Marie Colvin's Private War,"
Vanity Fair, August, www.vanityfair.com/politics/2012/
08/marie-colvin-private-war.

2. Colvin, Marie. (2012). "Final Dispatch from Homs,
the Battered City," *Sunday Times*, February 19, www.
thesundaytimes.co.uk/sto/public/news/article874796.
ece.

3. Gregory, Sam. (2013). "Co-Presence: A New Way to Bring
People Together for Human Rights Activism," Witness.
Org (blog), September 23, http://blog.witness.org/2013/09/
co-presence-for-human-rights/.

4. Bouchard, Stephane, Francois Bernier, Eric Boivin, Steph-
anie Dumolin, Lylene Laforest, Tanya Guitard, Genevieve
Robillard, Johana Monthuy-Blanc, and Patrice Renaud.
(2013). "Empathy Towards Virtual Humans Depicting a
Known or Unknown Person Expressing Pain," *Cyberpsy-
chology, Behaviour, and Social Networking* 16.1: 61–71,
http://online.liebertpub.com/doi/abs/10.1089/cyber.
2012.1571.

5. "Public Affairs Guidance on Embedding Media
during Possible Future Operations/Deployments in
the U.S. Central Commands Area of Responsibility"

(February 3, 2003), accessed June 3, 2008, www.
defenselink.mil/news/Feb2003/d20030228pag.pdf, Sec
2.C, sourced in Kylie Tuosto. (2008). "The 'Grunt Truth'
of Embedded Journalism: The New Media/Military
Relationship," *Stanford Journal of International Relations* (Fall/Winter), https://web.stanford.edu/group/sjir/
pdf/journalism_real_final_v2.pdf.

6. Tuosto, "The 'Grunt Truth.'"

7. Zelizer, Barbie. (2007). "On 'Having Been There': 'Eyewitnessing' as a Journalistic Key Word," *Critical Studies
in Media Communication* 24.5: 408–428.

8. Lynch, Lisa. (2013). "WikiLeaks after Megaleaks," *Digital
Journalism* 1.3: 314–334.

9. Julian Assange himself claims that WikiLeaks practices
"scientific journalism" based on public access to source
documents without editing or contextualization. It is of
course this editing and contextualizing that has historically been the core attribute of journalism.

10. Goodman, Amy, and Juan Gonzalez. (2013). "Glenn
Greenwald: Media Venture Will Empower Adversarial
Journalism to Hold the Powerful Accountable," *Democracy Now*, www.democracynow.org/2013/10/28/
glenn_greenwald_media_venture_will_empower.

11. Benkler, Yochai. (2011). "A Free Irresponsible Press:
Wikileaks and the Battle Over the Soul of the Networked
Fourth Estate," 46 *Harvard Civil Rights-Civil Liberties
Law Review* 311.

12. Dlugoleski, Deirdre. (2013). "We Are All Journalists Now: 140 Journos and Turkey's 'Counter-Media'
Movement," www.cjr.org/behind_the_news/turkey_
counter_media.php.

13. John Maxwell Hamilton and Eric Jenner argue that instead of seeing the death of the foreign correspondent, what we are really seeing is a new ecosystem in which the once-dominant parachute correspondent is now one among many. New members include the hired foreign nationals who cover events independently and then sell their reports to media agencies, local media that conduct international reporting from home, non-American correspondents whose work is available online through web-based publications, representatives of international organizations who communicate through official channels, syndicated news agencies that charge premiums for news, and, of course, amateur correspondents and witnesses.

14. Timothy Cook studies the media as an institutional actor. Through this lens the media are distinct from political actors, but in many ways they play a role like that of one large organizational actor. The media can be seen as a "fourth branch" of government, with its own role and responsibility, with the government playing a central role in its "product," or news stories. Institutional theory helps us to understand how different media outlets tend to report the same stories in the same way. Cook defines institutions as "social patterns of behaviour identifiable across the organizations that are generally seen within a society to preside over a particular social sphere."

15. Castells, Manuel. (2011). "A Network Theory of Power," *International Journal of Communication* 5: 773–783, http://ascnetworksnetwork.org/wp-content/uploads/2010/02/IJoC-Network-Theory-2011-Castells.pdf.

16. Singer, Jane B. (2005). "The Political J-Blogger," *Journalism* 6.2: 173–198.

17. Alfred Hermida, in a study of tweets using the #Egypt
    hashtag, similarly found that while some traditional
    media norms are replicated on Twitter, the people who
    decide what is influential are different—instead of an
    overarching media authority, influence was decided or-
    ganically by a mass audience. Hermida found four new
    norms that shaped the discourse around #Egypt on
    Twitter. First, there was an importance of, and constant
    desire for, immediate, instantaneous updates to the situ-
    ation, a sense that was embedded in the very language of
    the tweets. Second, traditional news sources, journalists,
    and citizens combined to form a Twitter crowd-sourced
    elite that was highly retweeted and followed. These elites
    interacted with each other, but the citizen and journalist
    accounts were more emotional and open than those of
    the traditional media. Third, there was a sense of soli-
    darity roughly determined by geo-location. And finally,
    and perhaps most critically, Twitter as an information
    platform allowed for a constant stream of information,
    which, relevant or not, contributed to the overall open-
    ness and liveliness of the news environment. This re-
    sulted in what Hermida calls ambient journalism, or the
    ability of consumers to immerse themselves in informa-
    tion about an event.

18. Castells, Manuel. (2007). "Communication, Power and
    Counter-power in the Network Society," *International
    Journal of Communication* 1: 238–266.

19. And as media theorist danah boyd argues, social media
    networks often mirror the power structures of the so-
    cieties in which they are grounded. Digital tools, she
    argues, are not representative of society as a whole,
    as they too are inaccessible to many. When the Kony

2012 video went viral, for example, it was not because of the power of the message or due to the decentralized acts of individuals, but rather due to an orchestrated campaign by the video's creators, Invisible Children, using a network of celebrities and university campus groups. People felt as though they were part of a movement, but the network had been heavily influenced by elites. It had structure. And that structure is a form of power.

20. Vicente, Paulo Nuno. (2013). "The Nairobi Hub: Emerging Patterns of How Foreign Correspondents Frame Citizen Journalists and Social Media." *Ecquid Novi: African Journalism Studies* 34.1: 36–49.

CHAPTER 6

1. Meier, Patrick. (2012). "How Crisis Mapping Saved Lives in Haiti," *National* Geographic, July 2, http://newswatch.nationalgeographic.com/2012/07/02/crisis-mapping-haiti/.

2. Zook, Matthew, Mark Graham, Taylor Shelton, and Sean Gorman. (2010). "Volunteered *Geographic* Information and Crowdsourcing Disaster Relief: A Case Study of the Haitian Earthquake," *World Medical and Health Policy* 2.2 (Article 2): 19.

3. Conneally, Paul. (2011). *Digital Humanitarianism,* November, transcript of TEDTalk, www.ted.com/talks/paul_conneally_digital_humanitarianism/transcript.

4. Meier, Patrick. (2011). "Theorizing Ushahidi: An Academic Treatise," *iRevolution* (blog), October 2, http://irevolution.net/2011/10/02/theorizing-ushahidi/.

5. As cited in Morozov, Evgeny. (2014). "Facebook's Gateway Drug," *New York Times*, August 2, www.nytimes.com/2014/08/03/opinion/sunday/evgeny-morozov-facebooks-gateway-drug.html?_r=1.
6. Meier, Patrick. (2011). "New Information Technologies and Their Impact on the Humanitarian Sector," *International Review of the Red Cross* 93.884, www.icrc.org/eng/assets/files/review/2011/irrc-884-meier.pdf.
7. http://mfarm.co.ke/.
8. Satterthwaite, Margaret L., and P. Scott Moses. (2012). "Unintended Consequences: The Technology of Indicators in Post-Earthquake Haiti," *Journal of Haitian Studies* 18.1: 14–49.
9. Romijn, H. A., and M. C. Caniëls. (2011). "Pathways of Technological Change in Developing Countries: Review and New Agenda," *Development Policy Review* 29.3: 359–380.
10. Romijn and Caniëls, "Pathways of Technological Change."
11. Stephenson, R., and P. S. Anderson. (1997). "Disasters and the Information Technology Revolution," *Disasters* 21.4: 305–334.
12. Nathaniel, Jordan. (2011). *Mapping the Sovereign State: Cartographic Technology, Political Authority, and Systemic Change*, Thesis, University of California, Berkeley.
13. Summerhayes, C. (2011). "Embodied Space in Google Earth: Crisis in Darfur," *MediaTropes* 3.1: 113–134.
14. Parks, Lisa. (2009). "Digging into Google Earth: An Analysis of 'Crisis in Darfur,'" *Geoforum* 40.4: 535–545.
15. As cited in Meier, Patrick. (2010). "Will Using 'Live' Satellite Imagery to Prevent War in the Sudan Actually Work?" *iRevolution* (blog), December 30, http://irevolution.net/2010/12/30/sat-sentinel-project/.

16. Harris, Paul. (2012). "George Clooney's Satellite Spies Reveal Secrets of Sudan's Bloody Army," *Guardian.com*, March 24, www.theguardian.com/world/2012/mar/24/george-clooney-spies-secrets-sudan.

17. Meier, Patrick. (2009). "US Calls for UN Aerial Surveillance to Detect Preparations for Attacks," *iRevolution* (blog), August 14, http://irevolution.net/2009/08/14/un-aerial-surveillance/.

18. Prendergast, John. (2007). "Museum, Google Zoom In on Darfur," *Washington Post*, April 14, www.washingtonpost.com/wpdyn/content/article/2007/04/13/AR2007041302189.html.

19. Hollinger, Andrew. (n.d.). "United States Holocaust Memorial Museum Crisis in Darfur," *Google Earth*, www.google.com/earth/outreach/stories/darfur.html.

20. Meier, Patrick. (2010). "Will Using 'Live' Satellite Imagery to Prevent War in the Sudan Actually Work?" *iRevolution* (blog), September 30, http://irevolution.net/2010/12/30/sat-sentinel-project/.

21. Heeks, R. (2010). "Do Information and Communication Technologies (ICTs) Contribute to Development?" *Journal of International Development* 22.5: 625–640.

22. Heeks, "Do Information and Communication Technologies (ICTs) Contribute to Development?"

23. Bedi, A. S. (1999). *The Role of Information and Communication Technologies in Economic Development: A Partial Survey.* ZEF Discussion Papers on Development Policy No. 7, Center for Development Research (ZEF), Bonn, May 1999.

24. Jonathan Donner and Marcela Escobari, for example, use a value chain model to show that mobile technology is increasing productivity in small enterprises and

helping them grow, but they find limited wide market effects. They conclude that in "value systems where mobile telephony is introduced, there is currently more evidence suggesting changes in degree (more information, more customers) than for changes in structure (new channels, new businesses)." Another study argues that a minimum threshold of ICT density is needed to see a positive effect on growth, that there is also a substantial lag time between the introduction of these technologies and a positive impact. A study for the Organization for Economic Co-operation and Development (OECD) urges caution on making direct connections between ICTs and productivity, pointing to a paper reviewing 150 studies on the topic published in the 1980s and 1990s, which showed a limited correlation. The challenge, the paper argues, is that it is very hard to disaggregate the effect of the introduction of new technologies from wider social and market forces. In this way, ICTs are better seen as a general purpose technology, which can enable new forms of production across an entire economy. Seen in this way, economists have found strong links within the US economy, but few such studies have been conducted in developing countries.

25. Alzouma, G. (2005). "Myths of Digital Technology in Africa Leapfrogging Development?" *Global Media and Communication* 1.3: 339–356.

26. Castells, Manuel. (1999). "Information Technology, Globalization and Social Development," UNRISD Discussion Paper No. 114, September, United Nations Research Institute for Social Development, Geneva, Switzerland.

27. Castells, "Information Technology."

28. Conneally, *Digital Humanitarianism,* 2011.

29. Collins, Katie. (2013). "How AI, Twitter and Digital Volunteers Are Transforming Humanitarian Disaster Response," *Wired*, September 13, www.wired.co.uk/news/archive/2013-09/30/digital-humanitarianism.

30. Palen, L., and S. B. Liu. (2007, April 7). "Citizen Communications in Crisis: Anticipating a Future of ICT-Supported Public Participation," in *Proceedings of the SIGCHI Conference on Human Factors in Computing Systems,* San Jose, CA (pp. 727–736).

31. Roche, S., E. Propeck-Zimmermann, and B. Mericskay. (2013). "GeoWeb and Crisis Management: Issues and Perspectives of Volunteered Geographic Information," *GeoJournal* 78.1: 21–40, p. 23.

32. Altay, N., and M. Labonte. (2014). "Challenges in Humanitarian Information Management and Exchange: Evidence from Haiti," *Disasters* 38.1: S50–S72.

33. Altay and Labonte, "Challenges," p. 52.

34. Giroux, Jennifer, and Florian Roth. (2012). *Conceptualizing the Crisis Mapping Phenomenon: Insights on Behavior and the Coordination of Agents and Information in Complex Crisis.* Zurich: Center for Security Studies.

35. "Foreign Assistance Briefing Books: Critical Problems, Recommendations, and Actions for the 112th Congress and the Obama Administration." (2011). *InterAction*, January, www.interaction.org/sites/default/files/2011%20InterAction%20Foreign%20Assistance%20Briefing%20Book_Complete_0.pdf.

36. Satterthwaite and Moses, "Unintended Consequences."

37. Zanotti, L. (2010). "Cacophonies of Aid, Failed State Building and NGOs in Haiti: Setting the Stage for Disaster, Envisioning the Future," *Third World Quarterly* 31.5: 755–771.

38. Alzouma, G. (2005). "Myths of Digital Technology in Africa Leapfrogging Development?" *Global Media and Communication* 1.3: 339–356.

39. Intel Corporation. (2012). "Women and the Web," www. intel.com/content/www/us/en/technology-in-education/ women-in-the-web.html.

40. Castells, "Information Technology."

41. One way to look at this internal access problem is through Jan van Dijk's argument that there are three class structures within a networked society. The first is the information elite, which are the highly educated, high-income group with nearly 100% ICT access and the ability to shape the production of the technology, either directly or indirectly. The second are the participating majority, which include the broadly defined middle class and they have near universal access, but not the same control over production. Finally, there are the disconnected and excluded, which have limited access. In a development or humanitarian context it is important to ask which groups are truly being served, and how programs could be exacerbating this divide.

42. Ndung'u, M. N. (2007). *ICTs and Health Technology at the Grassroots Level in Africa*. African Technology Policy Studies Network.

43. Rose and Miller as cited in Satterthwaite and Moses, "Unintended Consequences," 14–49.

44. Parks, "Digging into Google Earth."

45. Warren, J. Y. (2010). *Grassroots Mapping: Tools for Participatory and Activist Cartography*, Doctoral dissertation, Massachusetts Institute of Technology, p. 20.

46. Morozov as cited in Warren, *Grassroots Mapping*, p. 23.

CHAPTER 7

1. Clark, Campbell, Patrick Martin, and Mark Mackinnon. (2012). "Envoys Out as Canada Abruptly Severs Ties with Iran," *Globe and Mail*, September 7, www.theglobeandmail.com/news/politics/envoys-out-as-canada-abruptly-severs-ties-with-iran/article4526167/.
2. Petrou, Michael. (2013). "DFAIT Skirts Iranian Government, Tries to Reach Iranian People," *Maclean's*, May 10, www.macleans.ca/news/dfait-skirts-iranian-government-tries-to-reach-iranian-people/.
3. Tait, Robert. (2013). "Nuclear Deal with Iran a 'Historic Mistake,' Benjamin Netanyahu Says," *Telegraph*, November 24, www.telegraph.co.uk/news/worldnews/middleeast/israel/10470834/Nuclear-deal-with-Iran-a-historic-mistake-Benjamin-Netanyahu-says.html.
4. Nye, Joseph Jr. (2005). *Public Diplomacy and Soft Power*. New York: Palgrave Macmillan.
5. Nye, *Public Diplomacy and Soft Power*.
6. Pells, R. H. (1997). *Not Like Us: How Europeans Have Loved, Hated, and Transformed American Culture since World War II*. New York: Basic Books, p. 33.
7. Nye, *Public Diplomacy and Soft Power*.
8. Nye, Joseph Jr. (2009). "Who Caused the End of the Cold War?" *Huffington Post*, November 9, www.huffingtonpost.com/joseph-nye/who-caused-the-end-of-the_b_350595.html.
9. Nye, *Public Diplomacy and Soft Power*.
10. Khatib, L., W. Dutton, and M. Thelwall. (2012). "Public Diplomacy 2.0: A Case Study of the US Digital Outreach Team," *Middle East Journal* 66.3: 453–472. http://

cddrl.stanford.edu/publications/public_diplomacy_20_
an_exploratory_case_study_of_the_digital_outreach_
team/.

11. Khatib et al., "Public Diplomacy 2.0."

12. Public diplomacy projects under the Bureau of Information Resource Management's Office of *eDiplomacy*, www.state.gov/m/irm/ediplomacy/c23840.htm.

13. Khatib et al., "Public Diplomacy 2.0."

14. Miller, Greg. (2012). "Syrian Activists Say Pledges of U.S. Communications Aid Are Largely Unfulfilled," *Washington Post*, August 12, www.washingtonpost.com/world/national-security/syrian-activists-say-pledges-of-us-communications-aid-are-largely-unfulfilled/2012/08/20/14dff95a-eaf8-11e1-9ddc-340d5efb1e9c_story_2.html.

15. Glanz, James, and John Markoff. (2011). "U.S. Underwrites Internet Detour around Censors," *NYTimes.com*, June 21, www.nytimes.com/2011/06/12/world/12internet.html?pagewanted=all.

16. Hasan, S. (2013). *Designing Networks for Large-Scale Blackout Circumvention*, www.eecs.berkeley.edu/Pubs/TechRpts/2013/EECS-2013-230.pdf.

17. Hasan, *Designing Networks*.

CHAPTER 8

1. Schulz, G.W., and Amanda Pike. (2014). "Hollywood-Style Surveillance Technology Inches Closer to Reality," *Center for Investigative Reporting*, April 11, http://cironline.org/reports/hollywood-style-surveillance-technology-inches-closer-reality-6228.

2. Bacon, Lance M. (2012). "System Gives Troops 360-Degree Eye in the Sky," *Army Times.com*, April 16, www.armytimes.com/article/20120416/NEWS/204160317/System-gives-troops-360-degree-eye-sky.

3. Emspak, Jesse. (2013). "Wifi Tech Sees through Walls," *Discovery News*, June 28, http://news.discovery.com/tech/wi-fi-sees-through-walls-130628.htm.

4. Ward, Sam. (2013). "Infographic: How Facial Recognition Works," *Center for Investigative Reporting*, November 7, http://cironline.org/reports/infographic-how-facial-recognition-works-5516.

5. Borison, Rebecca. (2014). "This Security Solution Says It Can Figure Out if You Are Safe or Dangerous by Scanning Your Skeleton," *Business Insider*, April 26, www.businessinsider.in/This-Security-Solution-Says-It-Can-Figure-Out-If-You-Are-Safe-Or-Dangerous-By-Scanning-Your-Skeleton/articleshow/34213618.cms.

6. Metz, Cade. (2013). "Google's Quantum Computer Proven to Be Real Thing (Almost)," *WIRED*, June 28, www.wired.com/2013/06/d-wave-quantum-computer-usc/.

7. Der Derian, James. (2013). "From War 2.0 to Quantum War: The Superpositionality of Global Violence," *Australian Journal of International Affairs* 67.5: 570–585.

8. Bacon, "System Gives Troops 360-Degree Eye in the Sky."

9. Hambling, David. (2014). "Armed Russian Robocops to Defend Military Bases," *New Scientist*, April 23, www.newscientist.com/article/mg22229664.400-armed-russian-robocops-to-defend-missile-bases.html#.U3if-GFhdVgR; also see Tarantola, Andrew. (2012). "South Korea's Auto-Turret Can Kill a Man in the Dead of

Night from Three Clicks," *WIRED*, October 29, http://
gizmodo.com/5955042/south-koreas-auto-turret-can-
kill-a-man-in-the-dead-of-night-from-three-clicks.

10. Metz, "Google's Quantum Computer."

11. Schneier, Bruce. (2014). "Surveillance by Algorithm,"
Schneier on Security (blog), March 5, www.schneier.
com/blog/archives/2014/03/surveillance_by.html.

12. Human Rights Watch. (2014). *Shaking the Foundations*
(Report), May 12, www.hrw.org/embargo/node/125250?
signature=3b6d2513fd72d0b20ebb5d74af9dbb98&s
uid=6.

13. Amoore, L. (2008). "Risk before Justice: When the Law
Contests Its Own Suspension," *Leiden Journal of International Law* 21.4: 847–861.

14. Amoore, "Risk before Justice."

15. Schmitt as cited in Werner, Wouter G. (2010). "The
Changing Face of Enmity: Carl Schmitt's International
Theory and the Evolution of the Legal Concept of War,"
International Theory 2.3: 351–380.

16. Werner, 376.

17. Miller, Todd. (2014). "How We've Created a Booming Market for Border Security Technology," *Mother
Jones*, April 22, www.motherjones.com/politics/2014/04/
border-security-state-market-booming-technology?page=2.

18. Priest, Dana, and William M. Arkin. (2011). "A Hidden
World, Growing beyond Control," *Washington Post*,
September 30, http://projects.washingtonpost.com/top-
secret-america/articles/a-hidden-world-growing-beyond-
control/.

19. As cited in Stahl, R. (2010). "Becoming Bombs: 3D Ani-
mated Satellite Imagery and the Weaponization of the
Civic Eye," *MediaTropes* 2.2: 65–93.

20. As cited in Stahl, Roger. (2013). "What the Drone Saw: The Cultural Optics of Unmanned War," *Australian Journal of International Affairs* 67.5: 659–674.

21. Williams, M. C. (2003). "Words, Images, Enemies: Securitization and International Politics," *International Studies Quarterly* 47.4: 511–531.

22. Buzan et al. (1998:26) as cited in Williams, M. C. (2003). "Words, Images, Enemies: Securitization and International Politics," *International Studies Quarterly* 47.4: 511–531.

23. Williams, "Words, Images, Enemies."

24. Moskvitch, Katia. (2014). "Are Drones the Next Target for Hackers?" *BBC Future*, February 6, www.bbc.com/future/story/20140206-can-drones-be-hacked.

25. Johnson, Robert (2011). "Both Pakistan and Iran Say They Have Figured Out to How to Hack and Commandeer US Drones," *Business Insider*, December 16, www.businessinsider.com/pakistan-says-the-downed-helicopter-from-the-bin-laden-enables-it-to-hack-us-drones-2011-12#!Isddp.

26. Gorman, Siobhan, Yochi Dreazen, and August Cole. (2009). "Insurgents Hack U.S. Drones," *Wall Street Journal*, December 17, http://online.wsj.com/news/articles/SB126102247889095011.

27. Higgins, Kelly Jackson. (2009). "Researchers Hack Faces in Biometric Facial Authentication Systems," *Dark Reading*, December 2, www.darkreading.com/vulnerabilities—threats/researchers-hack-faces-in-biometric-facial-authentication-systems/d/d-id/1130382.

28. "Surveillance Cameras Can Be Hacked—Who Is Watching You?" (2013). *Info Security*, June 18, www.infosecurity-magazine.com/view/32991/surveillance-cameras-can-be-hacked-who-is-watching-you/.

29. Madrigal, Alexis C. (2013). "Stealth Wear: An Anti-Drone Hoodie and Scarf," *Atlantic*, January 18, www.theatlantic.com/technology/archive/2013/01/stealth-wear-an-anti-drone-hoodie-and-scarf/267330/.

30. Harvey, Adam. (2010). "CV Dazzle," *AH* (blog), http://ahprojects.com/projects/cv-dazzle/.

CHAPTER 9

1. Kapur, Devesh. (1999). "Processes of Change in International Organizations," *Conference Paper Helsinki*, http://dev.wcfia.harvard.edu/sites/default/files/164__Helsinki3.wcfia.pdf.

2. Falk, Richard. (2000). "The United Nations System: Prospects for Institutional Renewal," in *Governing Globalization*, ed. Deepak Nayyar, http://oxfordindex.oup.com/view/10.1093/acprof:oso/9780199254033.001.0001.

3. Meyer, Davis. (2012). "How the German Pirate Party's 'Liquid Democracy' Works," *Tech President*, May 7, https://techpresident.com/news/wegov/22154/how-german-pirate-partys-liquid-democracy-works.

4. Ford, Bryan. (2002). "Delegative Democracy," May 15, www.brynosaurus.com/deleg/deleg.pdf.

5. Meyer, "How the German Pirate Party's 'Liquid Democracy' Works."

6. Evans, Alex. (2013). "Avaaz CEO Ricken Patel's Commonwealth Lecture," *Global Dashboard*, March 22, www.globaldashboard.org/2013/03/22/avaaz-ceo-ricken-patels-commonwealth-lecture/.

7. Teleb, Ahmad R. (2014). "The Zeitgeist of Tahrir and Occupy," *TruthOut.org*, February 10, http://

truth-out.org/opinion/item/21776-the-zeitgeist-of-tahir-and-occupy.

8. Greenwald, Glenn. (2014, May 13). *No Place to Hide: Edward Snowden, the NSA, and the U.S. Surveillance State*. New York: Metropolitan Books.

9. "Embedded Governance: Downloading Laws into Objects and the Environment," *Life in a Computational Age*. Palo Alto: Technology Horizons Program, www.iftf.org/fileadmin/user_upload/images/ourwork/Tech_Horizons/SR1265EisP_Emb Governance_rdr_sm.pdf.

10. Diakopoulos, Nicholas. (2013). *Algorithmic Accounting Reporting: On the Investigation of Black Boxes*. Report, Tow Center for Digital Journalism, University of Columbia, http://towcenter.org/wp-content/uploads/2014/02/78524_Tow-Center-Report-WEB-1.pdf.

11. Leonard, Andrew. (2014). "One Code to Rule them All: How Big Data Could Help the 1 Percent and Hurt the Little Guy," *Salon*, January, www.salon.com/2014/01/03/one_code_to_rule_them_all_how_big_data_could_help_the_1_percent_and_hurt_the_little_guy/.

12. For a helpful discussion of algorithmic governance, see Barocas, Solon, Sophie Hood, and Malte Ziewitz. (2013). "Governing Algorithms: A Provocation Piece," *Working Series Paper*, March 29, file:///Users/taylorowen/Downloads/ssrn-id2245322.pdf.

13. "Unified Field: The 'Splinternet' Media Policy Project," London School of Economics and Political Science, November 18, 2013, http://blogs.lse.ac.uk/mediapolicyproject/2013/11/18/unified-field-the-splinternet/.

14. Meinrath, Sascha. (2013). "The Future of the Internet: Balkanization and Borders," *TIME*, October 11, http://ideas.time.com/2013/10/11/the-future-of-the-internet-balkanization-and-borders/.

15. Project MeshNet: www.projectmeshnet.org.

16. Project MeshNet: www.projectmeshnet.org.

17. Hodson, Hal. (2013). "Meshnet Activists Rebuilding the Internet from Scratch," *New Scientist*, August 8, www.newscientist.com/article/mg21929294.500-meshnet-activists-rebuilding-the-internet-from-scratch.html#.U1v768eLEi4.

18. Kloc, Joe. (2013). "Greek Community Creates an Off-the-Grid Internet," *Daily Dot*, August 19, www.dailydot.com/politics/greek-off-the-grid-internet-mesh/.

19. "ODDNS: Decentralized and Open DNS to Defeat Censorship." (2012). *TorrentFreak*, April 7, https://torrentfreak.com/oddns-decentralized-and-open-dns-to-defeat-censorship-120407/.

20. Benkler, Yochai. (2012). "Hacks of Valor: Why Anonymous Is Not a Threat to National Security," *Foreign Affairs*, www.foreignaffairs.com/articles/137382/yochai-benkler/hacks-of-valor.

21. McCarthy, Jordan. (2010). "Code as Power: How the New World Order Is Reinforcing the Old," *Intersect* 3.1.

INDEX